The Lo

Notes &

Queries

The Last Ever Notes & Queries

edited by

Joseph Harker

FOURTH ESTATE • *London*

First published in Great Britain in 1998 by
Fourth Estate Limited
6 Salem Road
London W2 4BU

1 3 5 7 9 10 8 6 4 2

A catalogue record for this book is available from the
British Library.

ISBN 1–85702–876–7

Typeset by Avon Dataset Ltd,
Bidford on Avon B50 4JH

Printed in Great Britain by
Clays Ltd, St. Ives plc

INTRODUCTION

So here we are, about to embark on *The Last Ever Notes & Queries*. 'Oh no!' I hear you groan. 'After nine volumes based on the weekly *Guardian* column, could this really be the end?'

Well . . . er . . . probably not. As we all know, it ain't over till the fat lady sings – whoever she was (see inside for details). And this title was chosen because, as we approach the end of the millennium, what more appropriate time could there be to look back at our most popular category of questions: when was the last . . . /who is the oldest . . . /what is the easiest . . . /etc etc?

So in the following pages you'll discover, for example, the last person in line to the throne; the oldest trick in the book; and the easiest driving test in the world (although the last of these is in some dispute, given our contributions from as far apart as Auckland, Massachusetts and Honduras).

Add to that a few more 'ultimates' – who first ate humble pie? which country is the most civilised? and how big must Noah's Ark have been? – and you should be getting an idea of the voluminous range and breathtaking quality of questions and answers for which Notes & Queries is famed. This may be said with a hint of irony, of course, but it comes nowhere near to the ultimate irony, which is revealed inside.

In the years since the Notes & Queries column began, it has expanded first into the globally available *Guardian Weekly* newspaper, and then into cyberspace, via its internet website (http://nq.guardian.co.uk). Hopefully it will continue evolving, just like the human race – or is this as good as we get, as one contributor asks.

And as the 2,000th anniversary of Christianity approaches, you may be wondering what happened to the last ever pagan to live in Britain. Well, don't worry – she's alive and well and living in London NW3.

So if paganism can survive for two millennia, maybe there is some hope after all that Notes & Queries can keep going for a few more years.

Joseph Harker
September 1998

QUESTION: When was food first preserved in tin cans?

☐ IN 1795, the French Directory, faced on all sides by the threat of military and naval action, offered a prize of 12,000 francs for a method by which food could be preserved in easily transported containers. It took the chef, confectioner and distiller, Nicolas Apert, until 1809 to develop a method for preserving food using bottles or jars sealed with wax and heated. His method was a success, but neither he nor anyone else knew why until Pasteur explained the science many years later. The tin can itself was invented in England in 1810 by Peter Durand, who used sheet steel coated with tin and soldered by hand. Both square, oblong and round containers were used. The English at this time thought that iron could solve most problems and it was natural that this refinement of Apert's process should develop in England. By 1813, Durand was under contract to the Royal Navy, and the patented cans were widely in use in the Navy by 1820. They were introduced into America about 1819, but did not really catch on until the Civil War made them essential.
D. N. Mackay, London N10.

☐ THE first patented can-opener wasn't invented until 1858, when Ezra J. Warner, of Connecticut, US, developed his device, based on the combined principles of the bayonet and the sickle. Until that point, people had used household tools to open their cans. On an 1824 Arctic expedition the explorer Sir William Parry took a can of veal bearing the legend: 'Cut round on the top with a chisel and hammer.' British soldiers, first faced with the new cans in 1812, resorted to using their weapons to open their cans. If they failed with their bayonets or knives, they shot at the cans with their rifles.
Karen Smith, Burnage, Manchester.

1

QUESTION: What is the origin of the expression 'jay walker'?

☐ As I was walking along, idly glancing through last week's Notes & Queries, I looked up to notice a bird that was walking boldly down the middle of the road, quite oblivious to the cars that were passing on either side. Need I say what kind of bird it was?
Christopher Reason, Hebden Bridge, W. Yorks.

☐ THE expression has nothing to do with the bird of that name. It is derived from the 13th-century French word *jai*, meaning a foolish or gullible person. This, in turn, comes from the Latin *gaius*. At the turn of the century in America, 'jay' was a popular slang term for a rustic or countrified person, whom city dwellers considered to be stupid and dim-witted. When one of these yokels visited the big city, his confused and dangerous attempts to cross the street were therefore known as 'jay walking'.
Edward Phillips, London N5.

QUESTION: Has anyone ever *seriously* researched time travel?

☐ A. J. W. DUNNE'S *An Experiment With Time* (1927) caused a sensation when first published. It proposed a concept of time in which time travel seemed possible. Max Planck could not fault Dunne's maths but said his premises were incapable of proof and so were unscientific. *Reverse Time Travel* (1995), by the scientist B. Chapman, explores the subject in depth and, while not ruling out time travel, makes it pretty unattractive. Of course, cosmologists have a deep interest in the arrow of time and the following works have information of interest to the potential time tourist: *The Mind of God* by Paul Davis (1992); *The Anthropic Cosmological Principle*

by Barrow & Tipler (1996); and *A Brief History of Time* by Stephen Hawking (1988). I hesitate to promote my own book, *Time Travel for Beginners* (2003) published by Farland Press.
Peter Sharp, Warkworth, New Zealand.

☐ I BELIEVE Margaret Thatcher had the British returning to the Victorian era. And not to forget that Curtis LeMay was bombing the Vietnamese back to the Stone Age.
Ken Frank, Claremont, California, USA.

☐ THERE is a fascinating (and readable) explanation of 'The Quantum Physics of Time Travel' by David Deutsch and Michael Lockwood in *Scientific American*, March 1994. It explains how although common sense may rule out such excursions, the laws of physics do not. It also rebuts some oft-heard criticisms such as that time travel can't exist, otherwise we'd have swarms of visitors from the future!
Tom Farrow, Sheffield.

☐ DIEGO Torres at the University of Sussex was quoted in various newspapers in March as having discovered 'worm holes' in the space-time continuum which may allow instantaneous travel to the farthest parts of the galaxy, as well as travel in time.
John Radford, Brighton, Sussex.

☐ A. J. W. DUNNE'S *An Experiment With Time* was not concerned with time travel, as Peter Sharp seems to suggest. It was an attempt to explain the sensation of déjà vu and apparent precognition. He kept notes of dreams and re-interpreted them to fit later events. His explanatory theory depended on the idea of time flowing like a river, on the banks of which the dreamer stood in Time 2, observing the flotsam of Time 1 events approaching and departing. This leads to an infinite regression of serial times, T3, T4, etc,

and conflicts with the idea of space-time within which events occur rather than being swept along by a current.
Martin Simons, Stepney, South Australia.

QUESTION: Who was the last Western head of state to fight in battle?

☐ THE last British monarch to lead troops into battle was George II at the Battle of Dettingen in 1743 during the War of the Austrian Succession. On mainland Europe, Napoleon III commanded at the Battle of Sedan in 1870, and there is a sad vignette of him in Zola's *Le Débâcle*, trying to expose himself to fire so that he might be shot and not survive his defeat. The latest clear example seems to be General Pilsudski, President of Poland 1918–1922, who commanded troops during the Russo-Polish War of 1920. In other cases the head of state is usually too remote from the actual conflict to qualify reasonably. The last European ruler to die in battle seems to have been Charles XII of Sweden in 1718, although one might include F. Solano Lopez, the megalomaniac dictator of Paraguay, in 1870.
Simon Corcoran, Cosham, Portsmouth.

QUESTION: What is the history behind the handicapping of racehorses? The human athlete after winning a few prized races isn't next lumbered with weights around their person!

☐ HANDICAP races – in which horses carry weights according to their past performance – developed in the 18th century as a means of giving each horse a theoretically equal chance of winning. This obviously attracts excellent betting and gives more owners a chance to win races with their expensive equine investments. The first ever handicap race was won at Ascot in

1790 by Seagull, a horse belonging to the radical leader Charles James Fox. The number of such races increased as bigger crowds demanded races with more than two or three runners. The Goodwood Stakes became the first surviving race of this sort in 1823, followed by the Chester Cup a year later. By definition, handicaps fail to sort out the very best horses, so more recently there has been an emphasis on strict weight-for-age-and-sex races, particularly the Classics. These – the Derby, Oaks, Guineas and St Leger – form part of the Pattern of non-handicap races, introduced in 1970 as a means of grouping European races into appropriate challenges during the season. However, many of the highlights of the jumping season are still handicaps – including, of course, the Grand National.

Hilary Bracegirdle, Director, National Horseracing Museum, Newmarket.

☐ BEFORE, during and just after the Second World War, track athletes *were* given 'handicaps' based on their previous record. Most were run under Amateur Athletic Association rules. At a meeting in Newcastle in 1942, I was handicapped at 36 yards (in front of a fictitious scratch man in an 880-yards race) and started between 14 and 54 yards behind the other runners. I actually won that race, but failed to win a mile race the following week, where I had to make up starts ranging from 47 yards to 99 yards.

J. H. Davies, Haslemere, Surrey.

QUESTION: Who gave the world's first benefit concert and what was it in aid of?

☐ JOSHUA and his trumpets at Jericho. The beneficiaries were Rahab the harlot and her family.

Ted Webber, Cairns, Queensland, Australia.

☐ AN EARLY example took place on 2 July 1944, at the Philharmonic Auditorium in Los Angeles. It was in aid of the legal defence costs of young Chicanos who had been arrested in what came to be known as the Zoot Suit Riots. On the bill were saxophonists Jack McVea and Illinois Jacquet, trombonist J. J. Johnson, pianist Nat 'King' Cole (under the pseudonym of Slim Nadine), guitarist Paul Leslie (aka Les Paul), bassist Johnny Miller and drummer Lee Young.
Mitch Mitchell, London SE20.

☐ HECTOR Berlioz gave many benefit concerts, usually for himself. He gave one in order to pay his wife's debts on 24 November 1833 at the Théâtre Italien in Paris. His wife, Harriet Smithson, was a British actress. An account of this concert is to be found in *The Memoirs of Hector Berlioz* (ed. David Cairns). Among other things, Liszt played Weber and the Fantastic Symphony had to be cancelled because most of the musicians went home promptly at midnight. The profit of 700 francs served to pay only part of Harriet's debts.
William Lyons, Solna, Sweden.

☐ TWELVE years before Mitch Mitchell's example, in December 1932 a benefit concert was held at the Rockland Palace in New York to raise funds for the defence of the Scottsboro Boys. These nine young African Americans, aged between 12 and 20 years, had been arrested in Scottsboro, Alabama, and, despite widespread belief in their innocence, sentenced to death for the alleged rape aboard a freight train of two young white girls. Charges were eventually dropped against five of them – the others were retried and convicted. Three of the four were later paroled, and a fourth escaped custody. The concert featured, among others, Benny Carter's Orchestra and a solo appearance by Duke Ellington.
Robert Greenwood, Chatham, Kent.

☐ BENEFIT concerts were held in the 18th century, the most famous being the first performance of Handel's *Messiah*, in Dublin on 13 April 1742. This was in aid of charities; later performances were held to raise funds for the Foundlings' Hospital in London. At the first performance, women were asked to arrive without hoops in the skirts, and men to leave their swords at home, so that a larger audience could be accommodated.
Denis Bates, Waunfawr, Ceredigion.

QUESTION: What is the origin of the phrase 'Scot-free'? Does it have anything to do with the Scots' reputation for not paying for drinks?

☐ ONE derivation of 'scot' goes back from modern French *payer son écot* (to contribute to common expenses) to the 12th-century Old French *escot* which meant the same thing. The origin of this word is the Frankish *skot* or tax. 'Scot' probably also has Scandinavian origins, from which it passed into Old and Middle English; and the phrase is found in the current and other forms such as 'scotch-' and 'shot-free'. Voltaire tells us in *Candide* (1759) of how the hero and his companion attempt to pay their *écot* after dining at an inn in Eldorado. Their offer is greeted with roars of laughter, because in this ideal land the government pays for meals in state-run hostelries. So they get off scot-free.
Charlotte Houlton, Morpeth, Northumberland.

QUESTION: When was the last man 'pressed' into the Royal Navy?

☐ THE Navy last recruited using impressment during the 'War of 1812', fought between Britain and the United States. Indeed, the practice was substantially the cause – ships of

the Royal Navy having been press-ganging British-born seamen from American vessels to fight against the French. Shortly before the American declaration of war, the patrol vessel HMS *Musquito* was found to be shorthanded, and intercepted a group of lobster boats off the German island of Heligoland – forcibly impressing Samuel Payne, an experienced fisherman, and John Thorogood, an apprentice. The men's colleagues sued for their release, and were granted a writ of *habeas corpus* – arguing that the Heligoland fisheries, possessed by the British since 1807, fell within a defined statutory exception. This incident illustrates how impressment differs from formal conscription into national service – being ad-hoc, arbitrary and (unless challenged in court) entirely undocumented. When, 40 years later, the Navy next fought a major war in the Crimea, the decision was made to proceed without impressment – and the success of this policy resulted in the practice falling into abeyance. However, the power (in occasions of need), to impress into the Navy any person of a seafaring character – excluding ferrymen and 'gentlemen' – remains within the royal prerogative; although the royal warrant to the naval authorities does not currently permit this power to be exercised.
Tom Hennell, Withington, Ches.

QUESTION: Is there a finite number of people in line to the throne? If so, who is last?

☐ EGBERT, who died in 839, is generally reckoned to be first King of England. Most English, Welsh, Scots, Irish, West Indians, Australians, Canadians, New Zealanders and Americans, together with a substantial number of people from Europe and the Middle East, will be descended from him. Several people have made valiant efforts to list all known royal descents, but without more than partial success. Even if we could list them all, getting them into the correct batting

order would present immense difficulties. The throne of England has often passed on pragmatic rather than theoretical grounds. Devising a rule which validates everything that has actually happened is not that easy. One vexed question is that of illegitimacy. Both Bloody Mary and Good Queen Bess were legally illegitimate at the time of their succession. Yet the claims of the Duke of Monmouth were rejected in favour of those of his uncle James II on the grounds of the Duke's illegitimacy. Today, allowing illegitimate descents would bring the descendants of Edward VII's illegitimate children (possibly including Mrs Parker-Bowles) in front of the descendants of his brothers and sisters, led by the current claimant to the Russian throne. However, one large group is barred by statute, that is Roman Catholics. So perhaps a symbolic answer to the supplementary is the Pope.
David Jackson, Coxhoe, Durham.

☐ *WHITAKER'S Almanac* lists 30 names in order of succession, the last being Marina, Mrs Paul Mowat. (My 1996 edition, however, omits the Earl of St Andrews at 19th, so perhaps Mrs Mowat should be number 31.) Anyone could expand the list by tracing the living descendants of Queen Victoria, also given in *Whitaker's*. They would, however, have to exclude Roman Catholics as ineligible.
David Matthews, Maesarfor, Ceredigion.

QUESTION: How high can a helicopter fly before the air is too thin for its rotors?

☐ THE maximum altitude which can be reached during forward flight typically depends more on the ability of the engine to breathe the thinner air than the rotor's ability to provide lift. Turbine-engined helicopters can reach around 25,000 feet. But the maximum height at which a helicopter

can hover is much lower – a high-performance helicopter such as the Agusta A109E can hover at 10,400 feet. However, if the helicopter remains in 'ground effect' – i.e. if it is hovering close to high ground – its maximum hover altitude will be higher. The Agusta can hover in ground effect at 13,800 feet. This is useful for mountain rescue missions.
Russ Swan, Lambley, Notts.

☐ SOME years ago the Soviet Union donated a helicopter to Botswana. The transport plane landed at the capital's airport (which is high above sea level), unloaded the helicopter and flew away. The helicopter was useless because it was already above its ceiling – it could not fly at all.
Garrett Simpson, Reading, Berks.

☐ GARRETT Simpson repeated an old urban myth about helicopters. The highest point in Botswana is only 1,491m above sea level.
Peter Wood, Blackheath, London SE3.

QUESTION: Who invented playing cards and what is the origin of Hearts, Diamonds, Clubs and Spades?

☐ PLAYING cards were invented by the Chinese before AD 1000. They reached Europe around 1360, not directly from China but from the Mameluke empire of Egypt. The history of suitmarks demonstrates a fascinating interplay between words, shapes and concepts. The Mameluke suits were goblets, gold coins, swords, and polo-sticks. Polo being then unknown in Europe, these were transformed into batons or staves, which, together with swords, cups and coins, are still the traditional suitmarks of Italian and Spanish cards. Fifteenth-century German card-makers experimented with suits vaguely based on Italian ones, eventually settling for acorns, leaves, hearts and bells (hawk-bells), which still remain in use. Around 1480

the French started producing playing-cards by means of stencils, and simplified the German shapes into *trèfle* (clover), *pique* (pike-heads), *coeur* (hearts), and *carreau* (paving tiles). English card-makers used these shapes but varied the names. Spade (pique) may reflect the earlier use of Spanish suitmarks, from *espadas* meaning swords, and clubs are what the Spanish suit of staves actually look like. Diamond is not only the shape of the paving tile, but may perpetuate connotations of wealth from the older suit of coins.
David Parlett, Streatham, London SW16.

☐ DAVID Parlett's explanation is most erudite, but surely a simple explanation is the four different ways of acquiring wealth: Hearts – marriage; Diamonds – inheritance; Clubs – war; Spades – work.
Hilda Handall, Prestatyn.

QUESTION: It is often said that the only man-made object visible from space is the Great Wall of China. How can this be so since, despite its obvious length, it is relatively narrow?

☐ THE Great Wall of China cannot be seen from space. However, due to dust storms a clear line is often visible from space where the dust meets the barrier of the Wall, so the astronauts can see its exact position. Major cities at night and large areas of reclaimed land such as those in the Netherlands are man-made objects that are visible from space.
Martin Lewis, Bradford, W. Yorks.

☐ THE world's largest building (by area of land that it covers) *can* be seen from space. The roof of the new Chek Lap Kok airport building in Hong Kong covers well over one square kilometre.
Steve King, Maida Vale, London W9.

☐ YOUR readers may like to refer to Arthur Waldron's *The Great Wall of China: From History to Myth* (Cambridge Studies in Chinese History, Literature and Institutions, 1990). Waldron points out that the notion that the Wall could be seen from the moon has been around since the turn of the century. He also traces the curious process by which the myth of the Wall, and its identification with China, went from origins in the gestalt of Western ideas about China, through reabsorption by flattered Chinese, to enshrinement in the most hallowed places of modern China's national iconography (as, for instance, in the lyrics of the national anthem). *Michael Radich, Matsumoto, Japan.*

QUESTION: Who started the practice of celebrating victory by spraying champagne over everybody within range?

☐ THIS must have begun as a Veblenesque demonstration of conspicuous waste, to show how rich one is. But a mere bottle of champagne is nothing to modern sports professionals – your Damon Hills and Ruud Gullits. To be truly Veblenesque, you would need to build a mansion and then pay the RAF to bomb it.
Robin Oakley-Hill, Sevenoaks, Kent.

☐ IN 1967, the underrated American driver, Dan Gurney, helped Ford to beat Ferrari at Le Mans. Presented with a magnum of Moët, the teetotal Gurney popped the cork and, at a loss to know where best to pour the contents, sprayed the crowd of enthusiasts and photographers.
John Winfield, Orston, Notts.

QUESTION: How fast would I have to travel to avoid being captured by a speed camera?

☐ As FAST as the law allows.
Myles Lawless, Cheltenham, Gloucester.

☐ SPEED cameras, or radar guns, work on the Doppler principle, that the electromagnetic wave/particles (photons) reflected from the moving vehicle have a lower or higher frequency, depending on direction and velocity relative to the observing radar gun. If the questioner travelled at the velocity of light, the photons would be unable to catch up with him, and thus could not be reflected back to the receiver, and no speed would be recorded. But to achieve this velocity would require infinite energy expenditure, and is therefore impossible for material objects. If his velocity of approach to the camera were near to that of light, the frequency of each reflected photon would be so high that its own energy, by Planck's Law, would be sufficient to destroy the camera, and hence the evidence.
Richard Harvey, Salisbury, Wilts.

☐ I RECOMMEND 125 mph. On my regular trips to London I do this most of the way, while reading a book. After a few pints of beer I come back at a similar speed, often dozing off. I have never been caught by a camera and my licence is not in danger because I don't have one. The transport I use is very economical, too – about 10p a mile.
Adam Sowan, Reading, Berks.

☐ RICHARD Harvey's answer – almost the speed of light – overlooks the fact that the camera takes two photographs in quick succession as the vehicle passes over a set of evenly spaced white lines on the road. These lines cover, say, 10 metres, and the camera probably has a 1/500th of a second shutter speed which is adequate to 'stop' the motion of the

13

car and take a nice clear picture of the number plate. To cover 10 metres in less than 1/500th of a second would require travelling at a mere 1,800 km/hr (around 1,100 mph) – considerably slower than light but somewhat more than the current land speed record.

John Brice, University of Essex, Colchester, Essex.

☐ YOUR previous correspondents, Richard Harvey and John Brice, are both way off the mark. It is only necessary to travel quickly enough to avoid a clear image of the number plate being recorded. I believe that the shutter speed in conventional (i.e. 35 mm photographic film) Gatso cameras is 1/1,000th of a second (the more modern digital cameras can have much higher speeds, but in this country they are not used for legal reasons). If the vehicle travelled, say, half a metre during the exposure, no characters could be recognised. This equates to a speed of a mere 1,800 km/hr, or about 1,120 mph.

R. Swan, Lambley, Notts.

☐ To AVOID capture, place two washers behind the top screws that attach the number plate to the car. This will tilt the plate down and avoid it being read clearly on the photographic evidence and make you difficult to locate.

P. Constable, London E1.

QUESTION: What is the longest English word with no recurring letters?

☐ A WORD in which no letter of the alphabet appears more than once is called an isogram. The longest English isograms are uncopyrightable and dermatoglyphics (the science of fingerprints), both of which contain 15 letters. See Richard Lederer's *Crazy English* (Sawd Books, 1992) for more fascinating trivia.

Jonathan Brazier, Birmingham.

QUESTION: What is the origin of the expression 'to pop one's clogs'?

☐ THIS dates back to the days when wearing clogs was the norm in northern mill towns, and impoverished workers would take their deceased relatives' footwear to the pawn-broker's and sell or pawn ('pop') them for a few coppers – often to help pay for the funeral.
Bob Heys, Ripponden, Halifax.

☐ PRESUMABLY the idea is that the only clogs that could be pawned were those of the deceased: the living needed outdoor footwear.
Clive Vaisey, London SE11.

QUESTION: Old maps reveal a railway station near Waterloo called Necropolis. Who did it serve and how did it acquire such a strange name?

☐ FOLLOWING the cholera epidemic of 1848, two industrialists developed a huge burial site for London's dead at Brookwood Cemetery, near Woking in Surrey – far away from city-dwellers anxious to avoid infection. Bodies and mourners were transported by train on the Necropolis ('City of the Dead') railway to the new burial site, consecrated in 1854. It was a controversial project. The Bishop of London condemned the 'offensive' despatch of first-, second- and third-class corpses on the same train, while poorer relatives worried that they might not be able to visit their loved ones' graves very often because of the high fares.
Paul Vickers, Dorking, Surrey.

☐ THE funeral trains comprised ordinary carriages for mourners and special hearse vans for coffins. The cost of a

railway funeral varied: it could be several pounds. Yet the Necropolis Company gave paupers a decent interment in a separate grave for only 14 shillings (70p), including the fare. Special tickets were issued: returns for mourners and singles for the dead.
John Clarke, Chairman, The Brookwood Cemetery Society, Surbiton, Surrey.

☐ LONDON was not the only city with a Necropolis – one existed in the main burial cemetery for Sydney. This impressive chapel was open at each end, a large entrance for trains to deliver the coffins and the other for transport to the burial ground. It was surprisingly called Goodwood. When the city of Sydney grew and engulfed the chapel, it was removed stone by stone and rebuilt in the new capital city, Canberra, and is now St John's Episcopal Church. The windowless sides of the original chapel are now glazed.
Donald Scott, Blackheath, London.

QUESTION: Where and what was the original ivory tower?

☐ THE ivory palace in Psalm 45 (and elsewhere in the Bible) is probably that of King Ahab (869–850 BC). Ivory – for decoration rather than as building material – was used in the ancient Near East as far back as the 15th century BC. The reference to 'ivory tower' in the Old Testament's Song of Songs is not helpful, since it refers to the neck of the woman the writer is trying to impress.
Kieran Conry, Catholic Media Office, London.

☐ PRINCETON University's Graduate College tower, completed in 1913, became known as the Ivory Tower because

one of the benefactors was William Procter (of Procter and Gamble), the manufacturer of Ivory soap.
Jo Wood, Leicester.

QUESTION: There is a clip of film from May 1964 of Mary Whitehouse launching her 'clean up TV' campaign. In it she says: 'Last Thursday at 6.35 pm, I saw the dirtiest programme . . .' What was it, and was it turned into a series?

☐ THIS question was put to the lady herself on her retirement – and she confessed that she could not remember. Unfortunately, there was no barrister present to claim, as they would in a court of law, that there had been in fact no 'dirty programme'. In an episode of *Till Death Us Do Part*, Alf Garnett's friend, Bert, remarks that, after seeing Mrs Whitehouse complaining yet again about hardcore pornography on TV, he had sat up all night hoping to see some for himself, and was most disappointed when it did not appear. He went on to wonder how someone of her apparent intelligence could claim to be an expert on something which palpably did not exist.
Keith Ackerman, Tilbury, Essex.

☐ THE programme to which Mrs Whitehouse referred was *Between The Lines*, produced by BBC Scotland but transmitted nationally. It ran for six episodes. Mrs Whitehouse had viewed, I think, the first episode (transmitted on 30 April 1964 on BBC1 at 6.35 pm), which featured Tom Conti among others. The programme was billed as 'A series of light-hearted enquiries into matters of no importance' and was written by Chris Hanley. Whether any episodes from this series still remain within the BBC archives, or what it was that so upset Mrs Whitehouse, I cannot say and wish I knew.
Olwen Terris, Chief Cataloguer, National Film and Television Archive, London.

☐ I WATCHED the programme (*Between The Lines*, 30 April 1964) and remember clearly the part that made me switch off. An otherwise good programme was ruined by constant repetition of a bonking scene. The first time I was mildly annoyed because it didn't seem part of the story. After the third time I decided not to bother again. It was boring, unnecessary and offensive. This time, Mrs W. was right.
A. Lubin, Swindon, Wilts.

QUESTION: Classical literature has many allusions to lions. Were there lions in Europe and when did they become extinct?

☐ REFERENCES to lions in Greek myths such as The Twelve Tasks of Heracles are not to be taken as good evidence for the existence of lions in Europe and would have found their way there through a combination of travel and observation of other civilisations. Lions were not creatures found in the Classical Age of Greece (fifth century BC) and any references to them, possibly in Aristotle's fourth-century BC work *De Anima*, would have been through extensive foreign research in the Persian Empire which had links with Africa. Biblical and Roman references such as Daniel in the Lion's Den are far more likely to be grounded in fact, as Rome's third-century BC conquest of Carthage would have most likely opened trade routes through parts of Africa allowing the acquisition of lions.
David Bamford, South Chailey, East Sussex.

☐ DAVID Bamford suggests that the lion is uniquely African: it isn't. Nor is the European lion merely legendary: it survived in Thrace even in the second century AD, according to the trustworthy Pausanias, who was alive at the time. There may be later evidence; but, in any case, the Collins *Field Guide to the Mammals of Africa* says that in historical times lions

lived in every country from Greece and Sinai to India (where a few remain). So, though reluctant to cast Daniel into the den, the Persian emperor Darius could not plead local un-availability of the necessary livestock.
Mike Lyle, Llangynog, Carmarthen.

☐ CAVE lions lived in England and Wales during the Pleistocene era, disappearing about 40,000 years ago. There were still cave lions in Thrace and Macedonia until the time of the ancient Greeks. The lions that the early Christians were thrown to were Barbary lions (presumed extinct since 1922) which were brought over from North Africa; Nero kept a group of them.
Mike Meakin, Wimbledon, London SW19.

QUESTION: They say something will cost the earth. If I were a wealthy alien, how much could I expect to be invoiced if I were to purchase it?

☐ BUY it from Westminster Council. Cost: 5p.
Ian Spencer, Sheffield.

☐ DEPENDS on where you bought it, who from, and when. If you bought it in the UK, you could expect to pay a whopping 17.5 per cent VAT, compared with a far more reasonable sales tax in the US. If you bought it from one of those tourist-savvy places (on Tottenham Court Road, or Times Square, say), you might be able to get it completely tax-free, as long as you kept the right paperwork. And if you bought it in the sales just after the peak planet-buying period, you could probably get some more knocked off the initial price. Come to think of it, when is the peak planet-buying period?
Terry Shuttleworth, London.

☐ WHY would aliens with superior technology (which they have, since they travelled many light years to get here) bother with buying anything from us when they can just as easily take it from us? Does the expression 'As easy as taking candy from a baby' ring a bell?
Jan-Willem van der Horst,'s-Hertogenbosch, The Netherlands.

QUESTION: Who was the Green Man after whom so many pubs are named?

☐ THE Green Man appeared at May festivities hidden in a garland or bower of foliage or flowers in May Day celebrations based on ancient fertility rites. Also called 'Jack in the Green' who appears in churches and cathedrals, on jetties of Tudor and other medieval buildings, he is a figure of medieval folklore, a symbol of the coming of spring, rebirth of vegetation and tree worship. He is usually given a sensual face with foliage growing from the mouth and curling around the head, carved in stone or made from oak.
Moira Brown, Dringhouses, York.

QUESTION: I have heard professional comedians claim that there are only 11 jokes in the world? What are they?

☐ TOTTENHAM Hotspur's first team.
Sean Cronin, London N1.

☐ IT IS not 11 jokes, but 11 butts of jokes that can be listed. My own version reflects the proportion of male to female comedians fairly accurately. The wife; the missus; 'er; 'er indoors; 'er cookin'; 'er in bed; 'er trying to compete wiv the Blonde; the muvver-in-lor; the wife's mum; 'er mum; his penis-size.
Murray Weston, Stevenage, Herts.

☐ IF THE questioner were to attend my comedy classes at City University, he would discover there are 10 forms of joke category: misunderstanding/farce; slapstick and visual humour; innuendo, wordplay and puns; exaggeration; reverse; analogy and comic metaphor; inappropriate response; repetition; irony, sarcasm and black humour; mimicry, parody and satire; oh, and repetition. Needless to say, if you're Jim Davidson, ignore the above.
Marc Blake, London SW14.

☐ MAYBE there's only one, as the poet Robert Frost intimated when he wrote:
> Forgive, O Lord, my little jokes on Thee,
> And I'll forgive Thy great big one on me.
Malcolm Johnson, London SW16.

QUESTION: From November 1896 to May 1897, mysterious large airships powered by propellers and decorated with electric lights were reported flying in California, Texas, and the Great Lake states of the US. Who built these craft and for what purpose?

☐ IN APRIL 1897, Jon Halley and Adolf Wenke of Springfield, Illinois, reported a flying craft of a similar type, whose 'pilot' told them that it was a new invention flown at night to attract less attention. The pilot stated he had left Quincy, 100 miles to the west, only 30 minutes earlier – an impossibility for an aerial object of the time. Similar objects were reported in Indiana, where a crew were making on-the-spot repairs. The pilot was tracked down by the press in Martinville, where he made the statement that he had an airship in Brown County undergoing repairs. He stated he had three machines flying in central states of the US. Whilst many reports of the time are undoubtedly hoaxes dreamed up by local newspaper editors to increase circulation, there remain some tantalising unexplained facts. Also in April 1897, for over 30 minutes, a huge airship was witnessed by jurors, judges and lawyers who had gathered outside the courthouse in Harrison, Nebraska. It had a bright white light, coloured lights around it, and was oval-shaped with a box-like structure hanging from it, with a propeller at the stern. To this day, though well documented, there has been no explanation for the sights observed.

Chris Picknell, Littlebourne, Kent.

☐ I'M SORRY to say that these craft probably never existed. Considered to be the first widely reported UFO flap, this wave of sightings has been revealed, fairly conclusively, to be a string of hoax stories propagated by reporters and telegraph operators and enthusiastically endorsed by a then less jaded public. It's possible that their stories may have been inspired by genuine reports of unusual lights (but not aircraft) seen flying in the sky, but it's probably too late now to uncover the necessary details of each individual case. Like their disc- and triangle-shaped contemporary counterparts, the mystery dirigibles were then technologically a few years ahead of their time. Clumsy balloon flights had been made in Europe as far back as 1852 and by mid-1897 at least two airship patents had been awarded to American inventors, but it wasn't until 1900 that the first successful (and very short) Zeppelin dirigible flight took place in Germany. Again, like today's UFOs, balloons and dirigibles had long featured in popular fictions of the time such as Jules Verne's *Around the World in Eighty Days* (1873) and were also regularly depicted in drawings and cartoons of the time. The mystery airships would return in 1909, visiting countries as far afield as the USA, Britain, New Zealand and Scandinavia, but their origins still remain a mystery.

Mark Pilkington, West Kensington, London W14.

☐ SOME years ago I researched the airship reports which

appeared in the *Dallas Morning News* during April 1897. In one of several reports of grounded airships, the occupants identified themselves as A. E. Dolbear and S. E. Tillman. Both were real-life academics. One of the two had taken leave of absence during the period in question. Dolbear's publications include (in the *Boston Globe*, 1898) an article 'Will Man Ever Fly?', in which he predicted that man would achieve powered, controlled flight in the near future. One of the more interesting reports in the *Dallas Morning News* describes a night-time sighting of a circular object with lights around the rim, so the two forms of UFO – the dirigible and the disc – were already around in 1897.
B. J. Burden, Braintree, Essex.

QUESTION: At what speed would Father Christmas have to travel to visit all the world's children (say, under 11 years old) in a 24-hour period?

□ THE following was first published in America's *Spy* magazine: 'There are 2 billion children (persons under 18) in the world. But since Santa doesn't (appear) to handle the Muslim, Hindu, Jewish and Buddhists, that reduces the workload to 15 per cent of the total – 378 million. At an average rate of 3.5 children per household, that's 91.8 million homes. Santa has 31 hours of Christmas to work with, thanks to the different time zones and the rotation of the earth, assuming he travels east to west. This works out to 822.6 visits per second, so Santa has 1/1000th of a second to park, hop out of the sleigh, jump down the chimney, fill the stockings, distribute the remaining presents under the tree, eat whatever snacks have been left, get back up the chimney, get back into the sleigh and move on to the next house. Assuming that each of these 91.8 million stops are evenly distributed around the earth, we are now talking about 0.78 miles per household, a total trip of 75.5 million miles. This

means that Santa's sleigh is moving at 650 miles per second, 3,000 times the speed of sound. By comparison, the fastest man-made vehicle on earth, the Ulysses space probe, moves at a pokey 27.4 miles per second – a conventional reindeer can run, tops, 15 miles per hour.'
Miss Blanaid McKinney, Macduff, Aberdeenshire.

☐ THE question is completely hypothetical. Everyone knows that in reality Santa has many helpers who make it possible for him to visit all children.
Steve Dawson, Ipswich, Suffolk.

☐ IF FATHER Christmas behaves as a quantum entity (a santon, presumably), physics allows him to pass through many orifices (chimneys) at the same time. This is possible as long as no experiment is set up to observe him passing through any particular chimney (otherwise his wave function collapses and you end up with reindeer all over the place). All children are told that they must never attempt to detect santons, so the success of the scheme is a great tribute to the obedience of the children of the world; for this to work they must *all* be good. Having passed through all the chimneys at once, it *is* allowable to detect the santon field on a suitable detector. For photons, photographic films show, depending on the experimental arrangement, stripes or spots on silver salts. It would seem that santons are detected by pine trees and stockings, which register the collapse of the santon field as small piles of presents. The fact that presents never appear in stockings already occupied by a foot may be a consequence of the Pauli exclusion principle.
David Masters, Dept. of Computer Science, American University of Paris.

☐ FATHER Christmas no longer has to worry about such things. He's been banned from the skies for life for persistently driving with excess alcohol due to the glasses of

sherry left for him by thousands of expectant children. Rudolph, and the other cruelly overworked reindeer, have now been rehomed and are enjoying tender loving care.
N. F. Taylor, Birmingham.

□ MISS Blanaid McKinney and *Spy* magazine are wrong in assuming that Santa doesn't handle Muslims, Hindus, Jews and Buddhists. My six-year-old Hindu niece Parama – who lives in Calcutta and calls Jesus Christ Jishu Krishna – hangs a pair of white socks every Christmas Eve and receives presents from Santa the next morning. Perhaps, given his busy schedule, Santa does not have the time to discriminate among children on the basis of religion.
Dipak Ghosh, Bridge of Allan, Stirling.

QUESTION: If the dinosaurs had been intelligent enough to develop complex civilisations, could any evidence of this possibly have survived the 65 million years that they've been extinct?

□ DINOSAUR scientists may have predicted the catastrophe which destroyed their population long enough in advance to have built a huge spaceship containing a sample of the dinosaur ecosystem – thereby enabling a small community of dinosaurs to make a timely escape into the cosmos. Perhaps they will soon be back to reclaim their home planet.
Stephen Shenfield, Providence, Rhode Island, USA.

□ ANY complex civilisation could not exist without use of metals and many other minerals, and that means widespread mining. If geologically ancient shafts and tunnels had existed, we should have found some. For instance, in the stable, mineral-rich 'shield' rocks of Canada, Australia and southern Africa, 'fossil' geological faults well over 100 million years old are not uncommon; and tunnels – which would in time

have infilled through detritus and metasomatism, etc. – would proclaim their presence by unusual shapes and mineral assemblages. Even areas outside the stable shields would occasionally offer evidence bared by erosion and so on. Add the fact that we humans found eucalyptus still confined to Australia and New Guinea, ginkgo trees to China, and maize to the Americas, and it seems that the denizens of any 'complex civilisation' didn't even travel.
Len Clarke, Uxbridge, Middx.

□ CIVILISATION is not defined by the use of metals and minerals, nor by the corresponding mining associated with that. That's like defining civilisation as the obliteration of rainforests for the provision of toilet seats. Had dinosaurs been ecologically enlightened, the constructions of their civilisations would have biodegraded long ago and no evidence would remain. If civilisation is a product of the making and upkeep of societal laws, the dinosaurs' extinction might have been the result. Carnivores may have agreed to give up meat and herbivores ceased grazing out of sympathy with defenceless plants. Egg-thieving mammals would have been encouraged to go to rehab. The tyrannosaur would have laid down with the diplodocus and never got up again. We may have missed the first truly civilised end of an era.
Trevor Lawson, Amersham, Bucks.

□ IT'S NOT impossible that several so-called 'anomalous' fossils bear witness to incredibly ancient civilisations, although it is impossible to ascertain anything about such societies. At least two artefacts have been discovered in coal: an 'iron instrument' resembling a drill bit was found completely sealed in a coal seam in 1852; and a piece of gold thread was found in a rock eight feet below ground level in Rutherford, Scotland, in 1844. Two apparent pre-prehistoric nails have also been found: a 2-inch nail in gold-

bearing quartz (reported in *The Times*, 1851); and a 7-inch nail in a block of granite in 1845. In 1968, in Antelope Spring, Utah, a 2-inch thick slab of rock was split to reveal a 'human' footprint, wearing a shoe, in rock 300 million years old. This find pre-dates the evolution of the dinosaurs. Moreover the foot, whatever it belonged to, had trodden on a trilobite (marine invertebrates extinct for 280 million years).
Garrick Alder, Kempston, Bedfordshire.

□ IT WOULD depend on whether the dinosaurs could have achieved our level of technology. The natural processes of the Earth's crust would have destroyed much evidence. Fossils survive millions of years, so perhaps artefacts made out of composite materials such as carbon fibre could survive, although buildings would have been buried. The only sure way of leaving a trace of civilisation is to go into space. The artefacts left on the moon by the Apollo astronauts will still be there in millions of years' time – if they have not been removed by future tourists. The Pioneer spacecraft, bearing messages to beings it may encounter, will still be voyaging through the stars for billions of years.
Peter Stockill, Berwick Hills, Middlesbrough.

□ IT IS significant that all four of Garrick Alder's alleged artefacts found in rock date from 1844 to 1852. There was a fashion for such tales at the time. Thus the naturalist, Charles Waterton, writes in a letter in 1847: 'Last year a rogue brought to me all the way from Leeds, and offered for sale a toad in a lump of coal. I had heard by chance that there was a private manufactory of these prisoners carried on at Leeds and so I would not even allow the cheat to unpack his wonderful curiosity. He sold it afterwards to a simple bird-stuffer in York for the sum of 25/-.' (*Letters of Charles Waterton* (London, 1855).)
John Trappes-Lomax, Bury St Edmunds, Suffolk.

☐ GARRICK Alder's 'example' of a 'human' footprint in rock 300 million years old was known to our geological department nearly 50 years ago, when a young fundamentalist showed us an article in one of his religious magazines. So we wrote three times to the magazine asking for details, without reply. Enough said.
Len Clarke, Uxbridge, Middx.

QUESTION: After the establishment of Christianity in the Roman empire, how long did it take for pagan worship to die out?

☐ WHEN Constantine the Great issued the Edict of Milan of AD 313, Christianity became legal in the Roman Empire; but pagan worship was still allowed, and Constantine and his successors continued to use the title *'pontifex maximus'* – guardian of the Roman cults. Christianity may have been the religion of the emperors and of many urban populations, but the official calendar of civic ceremonies continued to be largely pagan – albeit that blood sacrifices were no longer made. Furthermore, as education continued to be conducted entirely through the medium of pagan classics – Homer and Plato – so the literary and academic world remained non-Christian, or indeed anti-Christian. As for the countryside, the population had scarcely any contact with Christianity at all. This pattern broadly continued until the catastrophic defeat and death of Valens at the hands of the Goths at Hadrianople in AD 378. Theodosius I, who succeeded Valens in the East, refused the *pontifex maximus* title – accompanied in this by Gratian, the Western Emperor – and effectively proclaimed the Catholic faith (as defined in the Nicene creeds) as the official religion of the Empire. Theodosius followed this by the prohibition of all pagan sacrifices; and when he was established as sole Emperor (following Gratian's murder by his own troops) a series of

edicts was issued in AD 391 and AD 392 abolishing all pagan cults and ceremonies – including, for instance, the Olympic Games. This ended explicit civic pagan ceremonial – although the events themselves often continued with a superficial Christianisation. Evidence exists for a continued underground existence for paganism among educated people (a series of show-trials of officials accused of covert paganism took place in AD 579–580 in Constantinople); while remoter rural areas, such as Sardinia and parts of Spain, were at that date still said to be unconverted. Paganism appears to have ceased to have any significant foothold only around AD 600.
Tom Hennell, Withington, Ches.

☐ IT NEVER did. In England after the fall of the Roman Empire the Anglo-Saxon invaders brought institutional paganism with them and, despite the return of Christianity with St Augustine, this Germanic paganism continued. In the rest of Britain, and in other areas of the Roman Empire, Roman paganism, combined with older native Celtic paganism, continued underground and can still be found today. Admittedly many modern pagan practices are recent imports from the East, or even made up, but the genuine survival of pre-Christian beliefs – for example in our Christmas and May Morning festivals, Easter eggs, superstitions, Hallowe'en, etc – is not in doubt.
Simon Chadwick, Oxford.

☐ AS A Pagan, I feel it is important to add that we are still a worldwide network of peace-loving people who practise healing, herbalism and forms of prayer to nature in one form or another. Our festivals celebrate life and love and we do our best to be grateful and protect the planet – this is the same as in Roman times.
Catherine Randall, Pagan Federation, London NW3.

QUESTION: Where will it all end?

☐ COSMOLOGISTS are presently pursuing the answer through observations of the value of Omega (the observed density of the universe compared to a critical density). The value of this parameter determines the fate of the universe: if Omega is greater than 1 the universe will collapse into a 'big crunch' (the end!), but if Omega is less than 1 the universe will expand for ever (no end!). Omega exactly equal to 1 means the universe will stop expanding at infinity (no real end). Present observational data puts omega between 0.3 and 1, while theoretical arguments advocate omega equal to 1. So, to answer your question, never!
Dr Bob Nichol, Physics Department, Carnegie Mellon University, Pittsburgh, USA.

☐ IN BILL Gates' bank account.
Frederick Borden, Berkeley, California, USA.

☐ FOR those who have faith in the Hindu philosophy – where it all began.
Dipak Ghosh, Stirling.

☐ In their book, *The Anthropic Cosmological Principle*, John Barrow and Frank Tipler speculate on the expansion of intelligent life in the universe. They say that for them the end state of the universe will be when our descendants in the remote future, or other intelligent beings, have expanded into all universes which could logically exist and acquired an infinite amount of information. When this happens, the Omega Point will have been reached. They conclude their book by saying, 'And this is the end.'
Peter Stockill, Berwick Hills, Middlesbrough.

☐ I HAVE no idea but I'm sure it will be in the last place anyone looks.
Tom Whitehead, Bury St Edmunds, Suffolk.

QUESTION: In 1984 a High Court ruling meant that the last mortal remains of Edward the Martyr, King of England, were deposited in a branch of the Midland Bank in Croydon. Are they still there and why?

☐ THE murdered king was first exhumed from Corfe Castle when healing miracles began to be reported at his grave, and he was reburied in a shrine at Shaftesbury Abbey, to be venerated by medieval pilgrims until the Reformation, when he was again disinterred and reburied in a secret location within the Abbey grounds for safe keeping. The estate passed into the hands of the Claridge family, and in 1931 the bones supposed to be those of St Edward were again exhumed. John Wilson Claridge wanted these bones, as the remains of a royal saint and martyr, to be appropriately laid to rest, and invited a number of Anglican bishops to receive the bones for reinterment. His offer was declined, and there was contact with English members of the Orthodox Church, who agreed not merely to receive the relics but proceeded to acquire a former chapel of rest at Brookwood, near Woking, for conversion into a basilica for the relics. Claridge's younger brother Geoffrey disputed through the High Court the elder's ownership of the bones and his entitlement to surrender them to the religious order, hence their sojourn in the vaults of the Midland Bank. The Attorney-General's Office became involved in the affair because of the relics' supposed royal origin, but was satisfied with the security arrangements at Brookwood, and allowed arrangements to proceed. There was a move afoot recently for the bones to be returned to Shaftesbury, but I am not aware of any such development.
Bruce Purvis, Salisbury Library, Wilts.

☐ FURTHER to Bruce Purvis's reply, the relics were originally enshrined at Brookwood on 15/16 September 1984, but returned to the bank vault in the Midland Bank, Woking, shortly afterwards pending a final decision on the ownership of the relics. I believe they were finally placed in the church (converted from a cemetery chapel) in 1986. The court case continued until 1995 partly because the Attorney-General tried to claim the relics for the Queen; partly because his Department took time to specify the precise security arrangements for the relics in the church; and partly because of the brothers' continuing dispute. The case was finally closed in the Chancery Division of the High Court on 31 March 1995 when the claim by Geoffrey Claridge (who by now had died) was entirely dismissed. John Wilson Claridge, who rediscovered the relics in 1931, died in 1993 and is buried outside the church where the relics now reside. The relics of St Edward, arguably England's least important king, have received a certain notoriety through this dispute. Ironically the security arrangements demanded by the Attorney-General make them the most secure bones in Europe; yet the bones of much more illustrious kings are just buried, or are lost, or are abroad.

John Clarke, Brookwood Cemetery Society, Surbiton, Surrey.

☐ BRIAN Purvis mentioned that a move was afoot for the bones to be returned to Shaftesbury. As chairman of the board, I would like to stress that, although we would welcome the return of the bones of Edward the Martyr to Shaftesbury Abbey, there was no official move for their return. The board's immediate concern is to build a new museum. The Abbey had strong links with the Royal House, and the exhibition will feature the stories of the Abbey's foundation by King Alfred the Great in *c.* 888 for his daughter, and Edward the Martyr.

Anna McDowell, Friends of Shaftesbury Abbey, Dorset.

QUESTION: Does anyone still produce cheap mechanical, wind-up watches, or do digital and quartz now rule for all time?

☐ I HAVE just bought a gent's mechanical watch manufactured by Sekonda from my local Argos store for a very modest £11.75. The catalogue description warned 'daily winding necessary', but if it is anything as good as its predecessor it will give many years' reliable service.
Jack Akrigg, Rickmansworth, Herts.

☐ I RECEIVED such a watch as a present after a visit to Kazakhstan, where I conducted the state orchestra. It is Russian, and the brand name is 'Vostok'. It is very reliable – except when I forget to wind it – solid, and surprisingly ornate.
George Kennaway, Leeds.

QUESTION: In the 1920s, did people perceive that the Liberal Party was on the point of near disappearance; and are conditions today similar with the Conservatives?

☐ THROUGHOUT the 1920s the Liberal Party was split between supporters of Asquith and Lloyd George, the party's last two prime ministers. It wasn't that people perceived that the party was on the point of disappearance, more that the Liberal Party pressed its own self-destruct button (division within the party and the scandals over Lloyd George's sale of honours), during a time when a credible Labour opposition was emerging. The key factor to the party's demise came in 1924, when Asquith agreed that his party would support the first Labour administration under Ramsay MacDonald, which was a minority government. Austen Chamberlain, a leading Conservative, stated that Asquith had '. . . sung the swan song for the Liberal Party', because why would the electorate

vote Liberal when it supported a Labour government? In the subsequent election that year, the Liberal Party was destroyed at the ballot box. As to whether we have similar situations in the late 1990s, who knows? Maybe the issue of the European currency will be the final division for the Tories, as the First World War in Europe was for the Liberals. However, I somewhat doubt it, as the Conservative Party is like a cold; there's no cure and it always comes back!
Tony Kavanagh, Heighington, Lincoln.

☐ IN 1924, Asquith appears to have believed that, by withdrawing support from the first Labour government, he could engineer an opportunity to form his own administration. He failed, and Tony Kavanagh is correct to see this as precipitating a serious electoral defeat. But as the Conservative government ran into difficulties, the Liberals appeared to stage a revival – winning a number of by-elections, reunited under Lloyd George and putting forward J. M. Keynes's radical economic policy proposals. In 1929 they fought the election on equal terms with Labour and the Conservatives, intending and expecting to form a government as the largest party. It was their failure then, taking 25 per cent of the vote and only 59 seats, that condemned them to 'also-ran' status. The key to their failure was the decline of their local party base, whose job is to maintain the electoral machine through regular engagement in local politics and local centres of power. By 1929, this had ceased to offer a distinctive vision of local public service and hence was unable to mobilise local support in a general election. What remains unclear is whether the political environment of the 1990s might support a party that campaigns nationally without a local party base.
Tom Hennell, Withington, Ches.

QUESTION: Mother Goose is celebrated in pantomime, and is recorded as having been buried at St Olave's Church, London EC3, on 14 September 1586. But who was she?

☐ THERE is a legend that this pantomime/nursery rhyme character was based on an actual woman from Boston, USA, named Elizabeth Goose (sometimes 'Vergoose' or 'Verti-goose') who is supposed to have written a book of children's rhymes in 1719. Elizabeth Goose's grave certainly exists, but there is no evidence that she did write such a book. The character Mother Goose was first associated with nursery rhymes in a book published by John Newberry & Co. in 1781 entitled *Mother Goose's Melody or Sonnets From The Cradle*. The oldest extant copy dates from 1791, but it is thought that an edition appeared as early as 1765. Newbury appears to have derived the name 'Mother Goose' from a collection of fairy tales published in 1697 by the French author Charles Perrault entitled *Contes de ma Mère l'Oye*. This translates as 'Tales of my Mother Goose', a French folk expression roughly equivalent to the English 'old wives' tales'.
Nick Spokes, Ilford, Essex.

QUESTION: Red brake-lights were visible on two different cars in the TV serial *Dance to the Music of Time*, set during the last war. However, I do not recall such brake-lights in the 1940s. When were they introduced in the UK?

☐ VEHICLES first used on or after 1 January 1936 had to be fitted with at least one stop light at the rear. Two brake-lights became a legal requirement in 1954.
Anders Ditlev Clausager, Heritage Motor Centre, Gaydon.

☐ IN JUNE 1959 we bought our very first car: a 20-year-old

Armstrong-Siddeley 16 Saloon which had been built in Coventry six months before the outbreak of war in 1939. It had two brake-lights set on steel columns well away from the body and on either side of an illuminated number plate.
E. T. Topham, Oadby, Leicester.

☐ In the 1950s I owned an Austin 12 which had been built in 1939. The rear lights (which did *not* indicate the approximate width of the vehicle) were immediately to the left and the right of the rear number plate; and behind the same red glass on each side was a brake-light.
Peter Degen, Chalfont St Peter, Bucks.

☐ Nearly all cars have had a red brake-light at the back since well before the Second World War. In the case of English cars, they usually only had one. This shared a 'D'-shaped lamp fitting made by Lucas with the rear light which also illuminated the licence plate. Fords had one lamp each side but, at least in the case of the small Fords, the same lamp served as rear light or brake-light, as dual-filament bulbs were not yet available. The D-shaped lamp started to be duplicated at the rear of British cars, in about 1938 or 1939, on Flying Standards, for example, but with a white reversing light on the near side instead of the red brake-light. Larger, more expensive cars had the whole thing, lights, licence plate, the lot, enclosed behind a glass window. In the early thirties, many larger cars carried a cluster of three – rear lights, brake-light and reversing light – over a square rear licence plate on the off-side. In the 1950s a new regulation made it necessary for all cars to have two rear lights and two reflectors. Brake-lights were also duplicated.
P. L. Bloom, Mill Hill, London NW7.

☐ In 1939, the law required vehicles at night to show side-lamps (not exceeding seven watts) indicating the approximate width of the vehicle, each side-lamp showing a white

light forward. There was no law requiring brake-lights. No doubt, during the wartime blackout, no new law requiring additional lights would have been considered. (Source: *Manual of Driving and Maintenance for Mechanical Vehicles*, HMSO, 1939). There was certainly no requirement for brake-lights during the first half of the 1950s – look at any of the location car-chase sequences in the old Ealing films, not a blink of red as any car pulls up in *The Lady-killers*. One of my own vehicles, new in 1955, was not supplied with brake-lights.
Mike Whitley, Whitstable, Kent.

QUESTION: I can't remember the last time I had a 'square meal'. Can someone explain this expression?

☐ TRY an Oxo cube dissolved in a mug of boiling water, and one or more slices from a pan loaf – that's cubic as well as square. Or two slices of bread, and a slice of that pre-sliced, pre-packed processed cheese. Or does it have to be palatable?
Mick Furey, Maltby, Rotherham.

☐ THIS is a naval term deriving from the shape of the plates on which meals used to be served at sea. A tour around the *Victory* (Nelson's flagship, now permanently moored at Portsmouth harbour) will confirm this and proposes that the plates were square so that a rim could be easily added to the wooden plates in order to prevent food spilling in high seas. However, why plates should be traditionally round, and when this practice came into being, is unclear. Surely it would be much easier to make and to store square plates rather than round ones?
Melanie Simms, Oxford.

☐ IN ANSWER to Melanie Simms, surely plates are round because they were commonly made of clay (or similar),

turned on a wheel or made from a flattened ball?
Cecily Roberts, Hemel Hempstead, Herts.

☐ A 'SQUARE' meal is a good meal, 'fair and square'. Ancient Greek had a similar idiom. People called a good man 'tetra-gonon', which meant 'four-cornered' or, most commonly, 'square'.
Janet Fairweather, Ely, Cambs.

QUESTION: Why is Birmingham the only city in Britain not to have a road, street, square, etc. in London named after it?

☐ BIRMINGHAM only became a city last century and was never a county town, so it was never the name or title of a major land-owning member of the nobility.
J. R. Tarling, Putney, London.

☐ J. R. TARLING is surely wrong to say that all cities except Birmingham are named after major land-owning members of the nobility? What about St Davids, Swansea, Ripon and Ely for a start?
Bryn Gwyndaf Jones, Welwyn Garden City, Herts.

☐ IT ISN'T. The City of Londonderry is also ignored.
Ade Dimmick, London SW6.

☐ PLACES such as Oxford Street and Leicester Square were named not after the cities but from the titles of the owners of the land on which they were developed: the Earl of Oxford and the Earl of Leicester. The lack of a Birmingham Street is therefore explained by the lack of a Lord Birmingham.
Linda Stewart, Petersfield, Hants.

QUESTION: Are there any areas on the surface of the planet where the process of fossilisation of organic material is beginning?

☐ YES, most notably in the remaining peat bogs of the United Kingdom. These form as centuries of organic material such as sphagnum moss gradually grows on top of itself with the resulting death and degradation of the ancestor plants. Through the analysis of pollen from core samples of peat bogs, scientists have been able to ascertain what crops were growing in the past. Also, at the very bottom of the oceans where there are enormous pressures and little disturbance, marine life will gradually sink to the bottom and, over many millions of years, become fossilised. There are other examples – such as coral reefs, mangrove swamps and coniferous forests – but in each case a lack of disturbance is probably the most important ingredient.
Liz Maidment, Chester.

☐ THE House of Lords.
Roger Darby, West Moors, Dorset.

QUESTION: If murder were entirely legal, would society descend into anarchy, or would we all be much nicer to each other?

☐ THOSE tempted to murder would not have to worry about arrest and prosecution, but they would still have to weigh up the risk of being killed in revenge by a friend or relative of the victim. In view of the imperfect functioning of the police and courts, private revenge would not necessarily provide a deterrent weaker than that of the law. This is how things work in many parts of the world – the Caucasus, for instance – even today. One problem is how to end the inter-clan blood-feuds that arise when deterrence fails. Another is how to protect travellers venturing far from their family and friends. The stranger is well advised to seek a local konak – that is, someone willing to take upon himself the obligation to avenge him if he is killed. So would we be nicer? Certainly to those whose protection we sought to win or retain. And we would take care not to harm others whom we knew or guessed to be well protected. But loners and socially marginal individuals might get short shrift, for who would bother to avenge them? *Stephen Shenfield, Providence, Rhode Island, USA.*

QUESTION: In the book and film *2001*, the hero survives a brief exposure to vacuum. In other stories, vacuum is instantly fatal and very, very gruesome. What would really happen?

☐ ALTHOUGH there would be a huge temperature gradient between the 37°C of the human body and the (almost) absolute zero of space, heat cannot be lost in a vacuum by conduction or convection but only by radiation; so you would freeze eventually but not instantaneously. All moisture on the skin and inside the mouth, throat and lungs would vaporise instantly. The loss of the residual air inside the lungs would cause oxygen to diffuse back out of the bloodstream, leading to unconsciousness and then death within a few minutes. Fictional accounts often describe bodies as 'exploding' but this seems unlikely – the body is probably constructed strongly enough to withstand a pressure difference between the interior and exterior of just one atmosphere.
Mike Hutton, St Bart's and Royal London Medical School, London SE5.

☐ MIKE Hutton doesn't answer the question. In *2001*, even if the shuttle-craft pressurisation wasn't already lower than one atmosphere, the astronaut would have been able to

gradually reduce the pressure in the airlock to about half an atmosphere before letting himself be hurled out by the rush of escaping air. All then depends upon him being able to reach the appropriate button before losing consciousness due to the sudden depressurisation. If he were able to do this quickly enough, the airlock would repressure without his help. It is unlikely, upon once again regaining consciousness, that he would suffer no ill-effects, but he would live to tell the tale.
Terence Hollingworth, Blagnac, France.

☐ IN 1956, whilst employed as a welder for the then Atomic Energy Authority, I helped make a pressure vessel. It was tested by a vacuum process. Meter tests showed that a foreign body was inside the tank shell. We cut open the vessel and found that someone had left a hammer inside it. The steel hammer head was removed, as was a very fine dust that was once the wooden hammer shaft.
Mike Mitchell, Failsworth, Manchester.

QUESTION: I have heard there is a word which means 'to not know the meaning of a word and to have to look it up in a dictionary'. Is there?

☐ THE word you are looking for is 'paramnesia', used in psychiatry to describe the phenomenon of not being able to recall the meaning of a word – and, by implication, having to look it up in a dictionary. I presume you did once know the meaning of this word but have forgotten it.
Colin Hall, Hawick, Roxburghshire.

QUESTION: Is it true that Berwick-upon-Tweed is still at war with the Russians?

☐ BECAUSE of its status as a disputed border city between England and Scotland, Berwick was listed as a separate entity on declarations of war and peace treaties. At the outbreak of the Crimean War, Berwick duly appeared as one of the belligerents taking on the Russian Empire, but in the Treaty of Paris, 1856, ending the War, Berwick was left out, hence the continuing state of hostilities. In 1968, however, Berwick decided to end this crippling conflict and signed a peace treaty with the Soviet Union (who gamely went along with the exercise). At the accompanying civic event the Mayor of Berwick is reputed to have assured the Soviet ambassador that 'from now on, the Russians can sleep safely in their beds'.
Tom Seldon, Liverpool.

☐ I HAVE been told that the same applies for Monmouthshire in relation to the 1939–1945 War. As there was some uncertainty as to whether Monmouthshire was Welsh or English in 1939, it was mentioned in the declaration of war against Germany – but not in the peace treaty of 1945.
Sheila Millington, Weybridge, Surrey.

QUESTION: Which country has the easiest driving test?

☐ ARGENTINA. In Buenos Aires you take the test on the local amusement park's 'bumper cars'. If you can crash into at least a dozen cars in the allotted time and walk away with a smile you can drive here!
Rich Coleman, San Isidro, Buenos Aires, Argentina.

☐ HERE in Honduras a driver's licence costs less than US$7 and takes 15 minutes to issue. No driving test is involved. A

voluntary written test of 20 questions earns you a $2 rebate. This, coupled with a total absence of traffic police, results in a driving culture that is best left to your imagination. The official minimum age for a licence is 18. In practice, children of 12 or 14 are to be found driving their parents and friends around, and most of them carry an official driver's licence.
Ian Cherrett, Santa Rosa de Copan, Honduras.

☐ MY NEW Zealand driving test consisted of a 15-minute drive around the block while chatting to the cop about the All-Blacks. Half-way through, and after no manoeuvres or even right turns, he said I had passed and we drove back. Incidentally, New Zealand has an appalling road safety record.
Martin Wilkinson, Devonport, Auckland.

☐ IN SOUTH Dakota (in the 1950s), the day I turned 15 I walked to the county courthouse, paid 50 cents, signed a declaration that I was not blind, and received my full driver's permit.
Tibor Pollerman, Schrollbach, Germany.

☐ THE small Greek island of Symi, near Rhodes, has a test that consists of driving from the clocktower along the straight harbour road to the town square, a distance of some 500 metres, turning the car round and driving back. One candidate has managed to fail nine times – the last time for stopping in mid-test to chat with a passing relative.
Steve Pinder, London SE23.

☐ THE easiest is (or was a few years ago) Afghanistan. There was no test because there were no driving licences. But equally one could argue that the test in Afghanistan, like Saudi Arabia, is the toughest in the world. Women are automatically banned from driving, and once you've failed

the sex test there's little chance of passing on subsequent occasions.
Glyn Ford, Mossley, Lancs.

☐ ACCORDING to the *Guinness Book of Records*, the driving test in Egypt used to consist of merely demonstrating the ability to drive a few metres forward and in reverse. It was made more difficult by the introduction into the test of requiring candidates to reverse between two cones. However, after 'severe cone attrition', these were replaced with two white lines.
Matthew Seward, London SW19.

☐ IN ECUADOR there is no practical test, only a written one. So who cares if you only have one leg, one arm and a squint but can write?
Stephanie Stevens, Quito, Ecuador.

☐ IN RURAL New South Wales, Australia, the local police run the driving tests. When I took mine in 1983 we started outside the police station and took the first left turn four times. As we drew up beside the police station less than two minutes later, the officer said: 'You've passed. I knew after 50 yards you know how to control a car.'
Simon Kaplan, Chapel Hill, North Carolina, USA.

☐ WHEN a friend got his US licence, all he had to take was a written test – 30 multiple-choice questions with failure below 80 per cent. As (i) they reused the question papers, on which the answers had been thoughfully marked, and (ii) there was no supervision, so people just opened their highway codes to crib, he was surprised to be told that it was very unusual for anyone to get 100 per cent.
Peter Bently, London N6.

☐ IN 1980 I accompanied my cousin to the Eleyele Testing

Ground in Ibadan, Nigeria. He was told to read out the registration plate of the car he was leaning against and subsequently told to drive his car through a path marked by tyres placed on the open field where the test took place. Meanwhile the testing officer, who had not even inspected nor got in the car, wrote out the 'Pass' certificate which he gave to me. Some years later, in Lagos, my test consisted of a multiple-choice Highway Code questionnaire and a drive through the Ikeja surburbs of Lagos. The questions and routines were along the same lines as in London today.
Michael Olawole Famakinwa, Dagenham, Essex.

☐ THIRTY years ago, in Canada, I passed my test ten days after my first lesson. The 'theory' questions were of this sort: 'Someone runs in front of the car. Do you: (a) swerve violently on to the sidewalk; (b) bring the car quickly and safely to a halt without endangering yourself or others; (c) drive straight on and risk injuring the pedestrian'. The practical lasted about 15 minutes and included an 'oral' hill-start. I then drove in Canada for five years and failed a test when I returned to Britain. My wife drove for five years in Britain, took the test described above, and failed it.
Alan Alexander, Glasgow.

☐ MY RECENT Massachusetts test took all of four minutes and involved turning right five times, observing two stop signs and the speed limit. No parking exercises or anything difficult like reversing or emergency stops. All with an automatic car too.
Gavin Fraser, Quincy, Massachusetts, USA.

☐ IT IS possible to avoid a test completely. An acquaintance of mine, who held an Irish provisional licence, spent a summer doing voluntary work in Tanzania, where the authorities considered his Irish provisional licence good enough to give him a full Tanzanian licence. On his way home, he stopped off in Germany, which was once the colonial power in Tanganyika. As a vestige of those days, Tanzanian driving licences are recognised in Germany and can be exchanged for full German licences – which my acquaintance duly did. Back home, it was then a simple step to exchange his full German licence for a full Irish one.

Michael Holmes, University College, Cork.

QUESTION: What would be the constitutional consequences if the heir to the throne declared he/she was an atheist?

☐ THE legalist would say that a non-Protestant cannot be monarch under the 1688 Bill of Rights. However, the Bill of Rights was basically a package of measures by the ruling class of the day to nail a monarch who could use such ideas as the Divine Right to rule in an absolute fashion. The requirement that the monarch should be a Protestant was so that he/she could not become a Catholic and ally him/herself with absolute monarchs of the day who tended to be Catholic. Becoming an atheist these days would not entail an abrogation of British freedoms and there could be a case for amending the Bill of Rights by an Act of Parliament to allow an atheist monarch. Having an atheist monarch would have an impact on relations with the Church of England, but Parliament could simply pass an act declaring that the monarch is no longer the Supreme Governor.

Patrick White, London N19.

☐ AS AN atheist, the new monarch could not take the oath, created by the Coronation Oaths Act 1688, by which he/she promises to maintain 'the Protestant reformed religion established by law'. And the Accession Declaration Act 1910 requires the new monarch to swear before Parliament that he/she is a 'faithful Protestant' and will maintain 'the

enactments which secure the Protestant succession to the Throne'. Parliament could try to repeal these acts before the atheist heir succeeded, but the existing monarch would have sworn the oath and declaration and so could not assent to their repeal. These are the only two acts in British law designed to prevent their own repeal. One way round this conundrum is the Baudouin device. In 1992 the king of the Belgians abdicated for a day to enable a designated successor to assent to an abortion law which the king found morally unacceptable. In principle, a British monarch could do the same. The second is to have the repeal bill ready for the monarch's death. In common law, the monarchy is never vacant. The lawful heir inherits all the monarch's powers immediately on his/her death, before being crowned or making the Accession Declaration. So the atheist heir could immediately assent to the repeal bill and lawfully become an atheist monarch.
Laurie Smith, Carshalton, Surrey.

☐ BY THE Act of Settlement of 1701, the lawful heir to the throne is the first in the line of succession of Sophia, Electress of Hanover, who is also a 'faithful protestant'. When the monarch dies, the proclamation of a successor must, therefore, pass over any declared atheists (or Catholics) in favour of their god-fearing offspring. Patrick White and Laurie Smith have correctly pointed out that this law could itself be repealed, but they overlook the fact that the British monarch is also head of state of other Commonwealth member countries – and, under the Statute of Westminster of 1931, no alteration can come into effect governing the British succession until equivalent laws have been passed in all affected legislatures. This was last done on the abdication of Edward VIII – when it took several months – and the Commonwealth is both bigger now, and less inclined to defer to British prejudices. In any case, there could be no point to the change. It is inherent in the monarchy's claim to rule that they embody the principle that the government acts 'by the grace of God' – so stated explicitly in all royal titles, proclamations and commissions. It would certainly be possible to re-express the fundamental basis of government on entirely secular principles – but there would then be neither need, nor justification, for continuing to employ a monarchy.

Tom Hennell, Withington, Ches.

QUESTION: Where did the term carpet-bagger originate?

☐ A CARPET bag was a holdall made of carpet material, and the story was that after the American Civil War northern opportunists descended on the South with all their possessions in a carpet bag, and soon became rich. The more difficult questions are why Southern racist propaganda about reconstruction became widely accepted outside the South, and how the term became common in Britain. Hollywood has a lot to do with both. *Gone With The Wind* depicts 'carpet baggers' and was enormously popular in Britain. The 'Southern revisionist' view of the Civil War and reconstruction was prevalent in films which touched upon the subject, particularly Westerns, until recently. The earliest such film, the silent *Birth Of A Nation*, was directed by a Southerner.

John Wilson, London NW3.

QUESTION: What is the origin of the phrase 'doesn't cut the mustard'?

☐ IN THE ninth century, when mustard was one of the main crops in East Anglia, it was cut by hand with scythes, in the same way as corn. The crop could grow up to six feet high and this was very arduous work, requiring extremely

sharp tools. When blunt they 'would not cut the mustard'. All this and everything else you could ever want to know about mustard can be found at the Mustard Museum in Norwich.
Phil Pegum, Stretton, Ches.

QUESTION: Was there ever, boxing apart, a codified British system of unarmed combat, particularly as regards the use of the quarterstaff?

☐ 'BACKSWORD' matches – combat with heavy sticks with wicker handguards – are described by Thomas Hughes in *The Scouring of the White Horse* (1859). These were evidently codified to the extent of being umpired, having timed 'bouts' and ending when blood was drawn. There were also some, apparently regional, rules about the acceptability of certain types of blow, the Wiltshire crowd crying 'foul' at uppercuts dealt by a Somerset combatant. Several forms of wrestling – including Cumberland and Westmorland, Cornish, and a type described by Hughes as 'elbow and collar' – which permitted kicking – were also codified before the mid-19th century.
Lyn Murfin, Leicester.

QUESTION: Only two countries in the world have regular trade surpluses, while all the others regularly trade in deficit. Since the total deficit far outnumbers the total surplus, where is all the money going?

☐ ORTHODOX economists do not consider balances of trade to be significant since, in one way or another, the markets will clear. But the best hypothesis is that the money goes to multinational corporations, which never have deficits, except in some limited national accounting for tax purposes. Money,

as we all know, is created by banks. Since something like 90 per cent of international capital flows is for currency speculation rather than investment, it may be argued that this money is not real – most of it exists only within the casino of world currency trading. If it is not real, then where the money is going is not a real question. Economics is now a science of illusion.
Joan Remple, Ottawa, Canada.

QUESTION: The name Jerusalem means 'city of peace' and Benidorm means 'sleep well'. Are there other similarly ironic place names?

☐ GREENLAND?
Neil Croll, Allestree, Derby.

☐ I GREW up in Buenos Aires, which means 'good air': true, perhaps, in the 1500s when it was named, but not quite the grimy, humid air I remember.
Alex Laidlow, London E2.

☐ GREAT Britain.
D. F. Reed, Eaglescliffe, Cleveland.

☐ PHILADELPHIA, PA, is the 'City of Brotherly Love', but you have a one-in-five chance of being the victim of a violent crime in any given year.
P. Sanderson, Glenloch, Philadelphia, USA.

☐ 'BENIDORM' doesn't mean *dormir bien*. It comes from the arabic word 'Beni' (meaning 'songs of'), like a lot of other villages in Valencia (Benitachell, Benimuslin, Beniarres). They all are old Spanish-Musulman sites.
Angel Ocon Gimenez, Valencia, Spain.

☐ BENI in Arabic does not mean 'songs of'. It means either: children of, sons of, family of or offspring of. This is due to people living in tribal lifestyles at that time.
M. Al-Ahmad, London W3.

☐ THE source of the name Jerusalem is disputed. While it certainly came to be interpreted as 'City of Peace' (from Hebrew *yrv* 'to found' and *shalom* 'peace'), the name probably originally meant 'city of Shalem', the latter being an ancient West Semitic god.
Peter Bently, London N6.

☐ IN REPLY to Alex Laidlaw: the name *Buenos Aires*, literally 'good airs', has nothing to do with the quality of the air we breathe – which isn't bad as big cities go because flat pampas and the River Plate, the widest in the world, help winds get rid of pollution. Before self-propelled ships, sailors had to depend on the right winds to reach their destination safely. So it was only fitting that, when the first Spaniards reached this (for them) remote place, they thanked the saint patron of seamen, Santa Maria de los Buenos Aires, or St Mary of the good winds, by baptising this city after her.
Roberto Asseo de Choch, Buenos Aires, Argentina.

☐ THOUGH there are mountains just outside Los Angeles, the cities of El Monte, Monterey Park and Montebello are all securely in the flatlands, while neighbours Claremont and Montclair are doubly ironic in that they are both in the flatlands and subject to the worst smog in the area.
Tom Schneidermann, Washington DC, USA.

☐ PASSENGERS flying in to Kai Tak airport might question Hong Kong meaning 'fragrant harbour' in Cantonese.
Dan Coulcher, London W2.

QUESTION: Why 'a different kettle of fish'?

☐ THIS is a variant of the far more common 'pretty kettle of fish', meaning a disagreeable situation, which goes back at least to the early 18th century. In former centuries a 'kettle' was a metal pot used for boiling liquids or cooking, and a fish-kettle was a common household utensil. The phrase 'a kettle of fish' was also used in northern England and Scotland to describe an outdoor salmon picnic, as well as the pot in which it was prepared, and the ironic figurative usage perhaps reflects the dismay of finding that something expected to be pleasurable is in fact the opposite. Only when the lid was removed would the contents be revealed.
Professor Bernard Capp, Dept. of History, University of Warwick, Coventry.

QUESTION: *Chambers English Dictionary* defines 'haplography' as 'the inadvertent writing once of what should have been written twice'. Is this the most useless word in the English language?

☐ AS A calligraphy teacher, I find the word haplography useful. When concentrating on producing good letter forms it is easy to make mistakes such as writing 'rember' instead of 'remember'. Its opposite is dittography: the writing twice of what should have been written once, such as 'critics' becoming 'crititics'. There is also the homoeoteluton, in which, when copying, the eye returns to the same word but in a different place – either omitting the words in between or repeating words already written.
Susan Moor, Sunderland.

☐ THE question brings to mind the infamous case of Smith

and Jones and their examination: 'Smith, where Jones had had 'had' had had 'had had'. 'Had had' had had the examiners' approval.' Presumably, had Jones known of haplography as a recognised disorder, he would have found the word most useful as a basis of appeal.
Stephen Marriage, London W2.

☐ THE most useless word is 'reasonable'. Used in the Housing Acts of 1985, 1987, 1993 and 1996, this word is supposed to ensure that leaseholders won't get ripped off by unscrupulous freeholders by the issuing of outrageous bills. This word is used countless times in the Royal Institute of Chartered Surveyors' code of conduct for freeholders: 'reasonable costs'; 'reasonable requests from leaseholders'; 'a reasonable standard'; and 'a reasonable period of time'. But only a court can decide on what is reasonable, and litigation costs an unreasonable amount of money.
Danny McEvoy, Brighton.

☐ I OFFER the following, from the *Chambers Dictionary*:
paneity: the state of being bread;
wayzgoose: an annual picnic for members of the printing profession;
stillicide: the right to drop water on somebody else's property;
haecceity: thisness, i.e. the quality of being this;
corsned: the practice of establishing somebody's guilt or innocence by seeing whether they are able to swallow a large piece of mouldy cheese.
Mark Harvey, Canterbury.

☐ IN THE same dictionary, there is the following entry: *taghairm*, n, divination; esp. inspiration sought by lying in a bullock's hide behind a waterfall.
Ray Hand, Abingdon, Oxon.

☐ İN OTHER languages, two possibles are: *riman*, the sound of a stone thrown at a boy (Arabic); and *tsujigiri*, 'trying out a new sword on a chance passer-by' (Japanese).
Joe Kerrigan, Marsh, Huddersfield.

☐ SURELY 'mallemaroking', entered in *Chambers' Dictionary* as the 'carousing of seamen in ice-bound ships'? After all, who's to hear them?
Richard Holt.

QUESTION: What does humble pie consist of, and who baked the first one?

☐ WHEN the posh folks of old Northumberland tucked into a tender haunch of roast venison, everyone else made do with the umbles, or offal of the deer. Umbles are at their best when baked in a pie with beef suet, apples, currants, sugar, salt, nutmeg and pepper. But even if you love the taste, eating this pie is an acceptance of second best. For the recipe, see Jill Harrison's *Tasty Trails of Northumbria*.
Kathryn Leigh, London SE15.

☐ A PIE made from the offal was called 'a numble pie' (from French *nombles*, Latin *lumbulus*, a little loin). By mistaken word division this became 'an umble pie'. (By a similar process 'a nadder' became an adder, and 'a norange' became an orange.) The superfluous 'h' seems to have been added, perhaps through error, before the invention of the phrase meaning to be humiliated or made to be submissive, with the implication that umble pie was the food of the lowly. People were certainly eating it in the mid-17th century. 'Humble pie' (with the 'h' but without the metaphor) occurs as early as 1648, while Peacock has 'numble pie . . . and other dainties of the table' in *Maid Marian* as late as 1822. Nobody is sure

whether 'to eat humble pie' is the result of further error, or a deliberate pun, though the latter seems likely. The phrase was in use by 1830 when it first appears in print in Forby's *Vocabulary of East Anglia*. Thackeray uses it in *The New-comes* in 1855.
Ramin Minovi, Moseley, Birmingham.

QUESTION: The spoof TV series *The Day Today* told of a secret tunnel between 10 Downing Street and Buckingham Palace. Are there really such tunnels in the vicinity of Parliament?

☐ CHAPMAN Pincher, writing in the *Express* in 1959, refers to '10 miles of reinforced tunnels built under London after the last war at enormous cost. These tunnels . . . are below Whitehall, Leicester Square, Holborn and Victoria.' *Beneath The City Streets*, by Peter Laurie (Penguin, 1972), provides considerable evidence for the existence of secret tunnels under London, some of which were started as long ago as the First World War. The most famous is the one deep below Goodge Street underground station. On one of the platforms at one end is an obscure notice which warns of a deep shaft. This complex of tunnels was used as a transit camp by soldiers on their way to Suez in 1956.
Ken R. Smith, Leeds.

☐ ON A tour organised by Subterranea Britannica in 1995, we visited a former MoD bunker directly beneath Chancery Lane tube station in central London. We could hear the trains overhead, and there was a lift shaft along which the station could be seen. There was one inconspicuous entrance in High Holborn, and another in Furnival Street.
Hillary Shaw, London SW16.

☐ THERE have been several rumours over the years about escape tunnels leading from Buckingham Palace. These include: a tunnel running from the palace under Green Park where, rumours suggest, it intercepts the Piccadilly underground line, allowing the Windsors speedy access to Heathrow Airport; ditto to the Victoria Line, which conveniently runs directly under the palace; and a shorter foot-tunnel to Wellington barracks just across the road. Most favoured, however, is the suggestion that a tunnel runs from Buckingham Palace under the Mall to a massive underground citadel, known as Q-Whitehall, which lies 100 feet under Westminster and Whitehall and extends as far north as Holborn. Evidence for this includes a huge extractor fan just outside the gents' loo at the Institute of Contemporary Arts – directly above the supposed site – which the ICA confirms is nothing to do with them. The ICA building is immediately opposite a huge top-security fortress building, on the corner of the Mall and Horse Guards Road, which is generally accepted to be the service access to Q-Whitehall. It is also known that a tunnel connects Downing Street to a massive atom bomb-proof bunker constructed under the Ministry of Defence building in the early nineties at a cost in excess of £100 million. It is also likely that this building connects directly with Q-Whitehall. Therefore travel from Buckingham Palace to 10 Downing Street should be possible if the need arose.

David Northmore, London N6.

☐ I THINK Ken Smith is wrong when he states that the Goodge Street underground tunnels were used as a transit camp during the Suez crisis in 1956. In November 1954 I stayed overnight at the Goodge Street camp, on my way to Egypt. But at the end of July 1956, on my return from Libya, I was billeted for a night in a school or church hall just off Tottenham Court Road. I was told that Goodge Street was no longer used and later found out it had been destroyed by fire

in 1955. I doubt very much whether it was made habitable in time for the Suez crisis in October 1956.
Ken Light, Milton Keynes.

☐ THE construction of the Jubilee Line is a highly visible and disruptive process, involving thousands of construction workers. If there really are 10 miles of reinforced tunnels below central London, how could these be built and remain secret? Who built them, or is this a secret too?
David Powell, London NW1.

☐ DAVID Powell implies that 'secret' tunnels cannot exist since we didn't notice them being constructed. But London Transport advertises what it is doing. Other utilities which build tunnels, while not necessarily being secretive, nevertheless create as little disruption as possible so as not to antagonise the public. London Electricity, for instance, has in the last few years built miles of three-metre-diameter tunnels under London. Did Mr Powell notice? How much more, then, could have been achieved by an organisation which sought to hide what it was doing? As it happens, we *do* know who built some of the 'secret' tunnels. The eight or so miles of tunnel, 5.5 metres in diameter, which link various places in central, east and south London, were built by William Halcrow. This system, which was later extended westwards to Shepherd's Bush, is also linked to the extensive system of tunnels in the Whitehall area (which may indeed have a connection to Buckingham Palace) and to the massive telephone exchange deep beneath Chancery Lane. All this information can be found in two books: *London Under London*, by Richard Trench and Ellis Hillman; and *Secret London*, by Andrew Duncan.
Geoffrey Taunton, Portsmouth.

☐ I CAN assure Ken Light that Goodge Street transit camp *was* open on 3 December 1956. I, and 200 other matelots,

stayed overnight there on our way from Devonport to Mombasa to commission one of Her Majesty's frigates. It was a grim place and stank to high heaven.
James Stewart, Manheim, Germany.

QUESTION: Suppose you could fool enough people into queueing around a building in a continuous loop with all of them believing they were in a normal queue. Would the queue occasionally jump forward as usual or would it do something else?

☐ THIS would depend upon the queue's density. If the people were too close together, nobody would be able to move – just as in a traffic jam. As people became restless and moved off to find a more promising queue, others would start to move up to fill in the gaps, and once the gaps became large enough the entire queue would start to move. What happens next depends upon the degree of dullness of mind brought about by the action of queueing and the number of extra people now attracted to a moving queue. The question assumes that every member of the queue is under the same illusion. What more often happens is that a queue forms next to, or even on both sides of, any knot of 10 or more people in a public place, hence the well-known British ice-breaker 'Is this the queue?' 'I think so.'
Jonathan Brazier, Sheffield.

☐ ASSUMING the people are British, until the free ice-creams run out.
Robert Pedersen, Saint Privat, France.

QUESTION: Which has been the most peaceful, and which the most violent, place to live in this century?

☐ THE most peaceful would be Switzerland, which was non-aligned during the First and Second World Wars. The most violent has been Cambodia, where under the Pol Pot regime, he and his henchmen murdered over one million people.
Harish and Chandni Shah, Harringay, London N4.

☐ THE most peaceful inhabited territory has been Antarctica – especially since the Antarctic treaty of 1961 which suspended all national territorial claims and commercial exploitation in favour of geophysical research.
Tom Hennell, Withington, Manchester.

☐ IT HAS been estimated that half the male population of Ukraine and a quarter of the female population perished in wars, man-made famines and political purges in the first half of this century. In 1921–2 three million Ukrainians perished of famine or disease caused by the upheavals of the First World War, the revolution and civil wars. The enforced collectivisation of agriculture in the early thirties brought about a famine-holocaust in which more than seven million people perished of starvation. During the Second World War, over three million Ukrainians were murdered in the German occupation. Millions of Ukrainians also perished in the ranks of the Red Army or in German prisoner-of-war camps. The famine of 1946–7 took the lives of two million Ukrainians.
Sources: *A Pocketbook Guide to Ukraine and Ukrainians* (Ukrapress, 1985); *Babi-Yar* by A. Anatoli.
Matthew Irwin, Dublin.

QUESTION: How can I estimate, in megabytes, the amount of memory in my brain?

☐ THE conversion of information into binary digits is a gross simplification of processes in the brain. A single, static well-resolved picture on a video display screen might need 1.5 megabytes in a machine's memory. If anything moves, this will increase – and that is just one scene. How many scenes do we remember throughout a lifetime? What about language, literature, maths, science, music, to say nothing of neuro-muscular coordination? Machines are mere extensions of brains, devised to perform set programmes quickly. Gary Kasparov is no more inferior to a chess machine than is a bicyclist to a fast car.
Michael Dearden, Carnforth, Lancashire.

QUESTION: Why is 'goose-stepping' so-called? I have never seen a goose move in that fashion.

☐ THE German *Gänsemarsch* means 'in single file' – anyone who has watched geese will know that they walk this way. Presumably, whoever first translated the German misunderstood which aspect of the soldiers' march was being referred to.
Susan Pomeroy, Harpenden, Herts.

☐ WHEN I watched my neighbour's geese they were not walking in single file, but progressing across the field in an arrow-shaped formation similar to that of flying geese. They were, however, walking with their characteristic straight-legged gait, in which the foot is held rigid and in line with the lower leg and lifted high before being placed. Although not the same, their step is sufficiently similar to that of the marching style that the term 'goose-step' would do nicely if one wanted to be derogatory.
Kate Viscardi, Essendon, Herts.

☐ OUR sanctuary has various water-birds, including Canada, greylag, barnacle, snow and white domestic geese. We have never seen any of them walking this way. However, one swan who is recuperating after a wing injury does a fair imitation of the 'goose-step'.
Marjorie Unwin, Outwood Swan Sanctuary, Surrey.

QUESTION: Many people have stone sculptured pine-apples adorning their gateposts or porch entrances. I have heard this originally was seen as a sign of wealth, although another version says it is a sign of welcome. Which, if either, is correct?

☐ IN THE 17th and 18th centuries it was traditional for sailors returning from a South Seas voyage to signal their return home by impaling a fresh pineapple on the gatepost. Over time, this gesture became formalised in stone – a kind of nautical 'Dunroamin'.
Joe Callaghan, Booterstown, Dublin.

QUESTION: When my young children asked where they were before they were in mummy's tummy, I could only come up with 'Nowhere'. Does anyone have a more satisfactory answer?

☐ THEY weren't anywhere, they were preconceptions.
Gordon Jackson, Hyde, Cheshire.

☐ HALF of you was inside mummy, half of you was inside daddy, then we joined those halves together and made the whole you.
Nicci Salmon, London SW6.

☐ You are contemplating the wonder of the creation of your children out of nothing; there was no 'before'. Whether you choose scientific language or religious language to express it, stand in awe of it.

(Rev.) Michael Hampson, Harlow, Essex.

☐ The questioner should introduce his children to gardening. Even young children can grasp the concept that plants produce seeds which, given the right conditions, can grow into plants. Children can then be told that they began life as a seed which 'mummy' produced inside her 'tummy' just as a plant produces seeds. They can then be told that they did not exist before the seed was produced, the same way as a plant did not 'exist' before its seed was produced. Later, the questioner could explain that the 'seeds' which mummy produces are called eggs, which are just like birds' eggs, but instead of hatching in a nest they grow inside mummy. When the children start asking about egg fertilisation, they are ready for the full unexpurgated explanation; for this, I am sure the local library will have a wide range of helpful books.

Angus Baxter, West Lothian, Scotland.

The Bible says (Psalm 139):

> For You [God] created my inmost being;
> You knit me together in my mother's womb . . .
> My frame was not hidden from You when
> I was made in that secret place.
> When I was woven together in the depths of the
>   earth,
> Your eyes saw my unformed body.
> All the days ordained for me
> were written in Your book
> before one of them came to be.

Rachel Kimmich, Brenz, Germany.

☐ AN INCREASING number of people are taking seriously the possibility of life before birth. Experiences people have, 'memories' of a time before physical conception, and the reports of significant numbers of mothers who speak of having felt, sensed or encountered future children before becoming pregnant (often including a dream of a child, that later proves accurate) can no longer be dismissed as subjective illusion. Life before birth is indeed a logical correlate to life after death. And those who listen without prejudice to what (especially small) children say may catch glimpses of a world which, to small children, is still as real as our physical world; they have only recently come from there. Might not knowledge of an existence before birth help us to make sense of our individual and collective human destinies?
(Rev.) Peter Holman, Freiburg, Germany.

QUESTION: What actually is the oldest trick in the book?

☐ ACCORDING to a satirical ditty ascribed to Seneca (Roman philosopher of the first century) on the death of Claudius:

> Mourn, mourn, pettifoggers, ye venal crew,
> And you, newer poets, woe, woe is to you!
> And you above all, who get rich quick
> By the rattle of dice and the three card trick.

Hugh Sinclair, New York, USA.

☐ THE oldest trick in magical terms is the cup and ball trick, which is recorded in hieroglyphics in an Egyptian tomb. Most countries have a version of the trick (the magician starts with three cups and three balls, and finally three surprise objects are produced under each cup). In Egypt the *Gulli Gulli* men end up with three live chicks, in Europe three lemons appear.
Steve Kliskey, Chelmsford, Essex.

☐ This is found in Genesis chapter three. A serpent made Eve eat fruit from the tree of good and evil, pretending that the tree was to be desired to make one wise.
Osmund Jacobsen, Torshov, Norway.

☐ 'And God said "Let there be light"; and there was light.'
W. Huntley, Barnet, Herts.

☐ Send me a stamped self-addressed envelope and a cheque for £19.99 and I will tell you.
Lee Wright, Winchester, Hants.

☐ Does the oldest trick in the book relate to the oldest profession?
David Stewart, Hitchin, Herts.

☐ Hugh Sinclair must have been mistaken in attributing to Seneca (first century) a reference to 'the three-card trick'. Cards were unknown in Europe until the 14th century.
Trevor Denning, Birmingham.

QUESTION: Why 'bubble and squeak'?

☐ My gran says that they used to make it from brussels and swede, possibly resulting in the similar sounding name.
Ralph Doane, Freshwater, Isle of Wight.

☐ When cold boiled potatoes and greens are fried together (sometimes with meat) they first *bubble* in water on boiling and afterwards *squeak* in the frying pan.
Richard Webber, Bristol.

☐ Onomatopoeia, my dear reader. 'Bubble' from the sound emitted by frying mashed potato, cabbage and onions

together. 'Squeak' from the sound caused by (in)digestion on the part of the eater.
Miriam Ross, Gravesend, Kent.

QUESTION: When were the first fountains made and how were they operated?

☐ AN EARLY example of a fountain, found in Mesopotamia, dates from around 3000 BC. It consisted of a series of basins which made use of a natural spring. A similar system is found in Greek and Roman remains. Mechanically operated fountains became familiar during the 15th century in Italy. (Source: *The Origins of Everything*, by Gordon Grimley, 1973.)
Ivor Solomons, Norwich.

☐ FURTHER to Ivor Solomons' reply: growing interest in the use of water in the new grand gardens of 16th- and 17th-century Italy is attributed by Simon Schama (*Landscape and Memory*, 1995) to the publication in Venice in 1499 of *The Dream of Poliphilus* by Francesco Colonna. He drew on classical and pagan tradition to develop a mythical world in which water in general, and fountains in particular, played an important role. This dream was made concrete by the architects of Roman and Tuscan villas in the mid and late 16th century, where fountains were conceived as 'stations en route to illumination'. The 'new' technology of hydro-mechanics, employed to produce the fountains and special effects, was developed by *fontanieri*, whose talents had to combine mastery of both physics and metaphysics. Schama says that this knowledge was drawn from the writings of two physicist-mathematicians, Ctesibius and Hero, working in Alexandria in the third century BC. They were aware of the expanding properties of water under heat and had experimented with the effects of air pressure and controlled

vacuums in order to produce decorative water-works. This work was known during the Middle Ages through manuscripts in Latin and Arabic and was published in Italian during the 16th century. The Italian *fontanieri* were soon called on by royalty in France, England and Austria to apply their expertise to their own palaces and to develop the technology for public works including the supply of clean water.
Peter Mackay, London SE10.

QUESTION: When does a cult become a religion?

☐ WHEN it is granted a tax-free status by the Government.
Anthony Breckner, London W4.

☐ WHEN it progresses from killing its members to killing non-members.
David Lewin, Oxford.

☐ THE essential difference is openness. Religions publish their beliefs openly in the Bible, Koran, Bhagavadgita, etc., and seek to persuade the public of their truth. Anyone who accepts these beliefs and the accompanying rituals is recognised as a member of the religion. There is a priesthood which is open to any (normally male) person with the necessary commitment. Religions therefore seek a mass following. Cults, however, rely on secret or special knowledge which is revealed only to initiates by the cult's founder or his/her chosen representatives. Beliefs aren't normally published. Everything depends on a personal relationship between the founder and followers, who are required to separate themselves from the rest of the world. This enables the founder and his associates to dominate and exploit the members. All religions begin as cults. Christianity began as one of several competing messianic sects and became a

religion when Paul and his followers began proselytising outside Judea. Cults fade away when those who knew the founder die. Who remembers the Ranters, the Sandemanians or the Muggletonians now?
Laurie Smith, Carshalton, Surrey.

QUESTION: Henry Mayhew's book *London Labour and the London Poor* mentions a Professor Sands, who walked on ceilings using an 'air-exhausting boot', on the model of a fly's foot. Did such a person exist and, if so, how did the boot work?

☐ THE American Richard Sands introduced the ceiling act to his Sands' American Circus in 1852. He walked upside down on a nine-foot marble slab suspended about 20 feet above the ground. Later that year he is reported to have presented his ceiling-walking at the Surrey Theatre, and at Drury Lane in 1853, using rubber suction pads attached to his feet. Henry Mayhew's informant suggested that the performer he saw was not the real Sands because he was killed on his benefit night in America. One version claims that this happened at Melrose, Massachusetts, in 1861. (Ceiling-walking in the town hall, a section of the plaster came away and he fell and broke his neck.) Another source says that Richard Sands died in Havana, Cuba. There were a number of ceiling walkers in 19th-century Britain. A number used the suction pad method, which required a very smooth surface, but most used a system of hooks and rings, at such a height that the aids were invisible.
John Turner, Circus Friends Association, Formby, Merseyside.

QUESTION: I had the impression that the adjective 'unique' was an absolute. As it is now frequently qualified by an adverb, is it now somehow 'less unique' than it used to be?

☐ ALMOST definitely.
Nik Devlin, Glasgow.

☐ THE usage of 'fairly unique' is becoming increasingly ubiquitous, and the prevalence of unqualified absolutes, once so essential to our language, is today extremely minimal. People now seem to be fairly unanimous in thinking that this very specific grammatical idea, hitherto considered highly necessary, is becoming more and more extinct. I have recently read of an 'extremely invulnerable' aircraft carrier, and also of a 'final ultimatum'. While the latter may not count as a qualified absolute, it is rather tautologous, if not in the least ambiguous. My very central concern is that the highly current practice of qualifying to a degree an absolute is now so endemic that one would be most mistaken to describe it as wrong.
Terry Richter, Walderton, Chichester.

☐ THE *Oxford English Dictionary* lists a second, though disputed, meaning of 'unusual, remarkable'. As English grammar, and the contents of the *OED*, is determined by usage and not by a set of fixed rules, we'll just have to accept that 'unique' is *not* as unique as it once was.
Valerie Antcliffe, Huddersfield.

QUESTION: What are the three greatest conspiracies of all time?

☐ CHRISTIANITY, Judaism and Islam.
Norman Temple, Edmonton, Canada.

☐ As FAR as this country is concerned, and bearing in mind long-term effects, how about: privatisation; share options; and remuneration committees?
Len Feltham, Keynsham, Bristol.

☐ THE *Oxford Dictionary* defines conspiracy as a 'combination of people for an unlawful or immoral purpose'. Three candidates:
(1) The slave trade. Since it continued for some two and a half centuries, this is also the longest conspiracy in history. The British were probably the worst offenders.
(2) The Holocaust. The fact that this was, indeed, a broadly based German conspiracy is only now being revealed.
(3) The rape of Zaire. The process was started by the Belgians, with great brutality, in the late 19th century. After independence was continued by Mobutu's clique, with the support of Western commercial and political interests. One of Africa's richest countries is now bankrupt.
Martin Ballard, Cambridge.

☐ RELIGION, masonry, and Manchester United.
George Bigby, Tarporley, Cheshire.

☐ FIRST: the Masonic Ripper, as promoted by Stephen Knight. Jack the Ripper was a gang of three men employed by members of the British government to murder a group of prostitutes, one of whom had given birth to a royal bastard. The various mutilations inflicted were a coded warning to others. Second: the systematic (and continuing) effort to shield those responsible for murdering President Kennedy. Third: that'd be telling. The greatest conspiracy of all was/will be 100 per cent successful and will never be discovered.
G. Alder, Leicester.

☐ WHILE I wouldn't contest Martin Ballard's choices, his use

69

of dictionary definition is too broad. The *OED* defines the *verb* more precisely: 'to combine *privily* to do something criminal, illegal, or reprehensible (esp. *to commit treason* or murder, excite sedition, etc.).' The words I've emphasised point clearly to the Gunpowder Plot of 1605. And if you tend towards the interpretation that the whole thing was instigated by James I's secretary of state, Robert Cecil, in order to legitimate a Catholic purge, and that the executed 'conspirators' were falsely promised an amnesty for their participation – this is surely the single greatest conspiracy of them all.
Tony Walton, Hove, East Sussex.

□ LEASEHOLD abuse. Brought about by loopholes in legislation discovered in the early nineties by rapacious freeholders, thousands of UK citizens have been bled dry financially. This is pay for non-existent 'services'. In truth it is to pay for the expensive tastes in vehicles that freeholders seem to have. Non-payment has resulted, until very recently, in leaseholders losing their homes to the freeholder and still having a mortgage to pay. Government members are slow to change legislation because their friends are often rich freeholders. Solicitors and surveyors like it because they get lots of business, much of which involves long, complicated cases. Builders think it's great because they can do lots of work, often shoddy so it has to be done again in a couple of years. Sounds like conspiracy to me.
Danny McEvoy, Brighton.

□ YOUR answers so far show how successful the really great conspiracies are. The first is the conspiracy to make nuclear bomb fuel at Dounreay along with a secret agreement with the United States, who swapped the nuclear fuel for enriched uranium. But all nuclear reactors make plutonium – it's an inevitable part of the molecular reaction – so that all Europe and Russia are now awash with nuclear bombs capable of

destroying all humanity. The next is the secret change made by the world treasuries to convert the assumption of 'inflation', from the fraudulent increase and issue of banks' paper finances, into the average of the retail prices of a list of shopping goods from stores. There is no public statement of the goods listed, there is no stated government treasury department who agreed the lists, there are no listed money values for the 446 items on the list for the average 'inflation', and there is no challenge to the average, or methods used to get it. The next is the secret assumptions of the gross domestic product. Who decides? What product qualifies for the GDP? And what part of the public works is in the GDP? It is all a secret and again wangled by the government's treasuries. The GDP is in agreement for the countries of the EU plus the USA, Canada, Mexico, Bolivia and Argentina and thus must be a serious conspiracy because the top permanent civil missions must have all agreed. But possibly the worst conspiracy is the one to hide the continuous systems of payments of inter-country debt for the payments of all debts for all goods sold between all countries. Where does the 'money' originate from and how is it issued?
John D. Berridge, Whitchurch, Cardiff.

☐ I COULD tell you, but I'd have to kill you afterwards.
Carl Zetie, Redwood Shores, California, USA.

QUESTION: Is there any town in Britain which doesn't have at least some claim to fame: about which no superlative can be said, which has never had any famous resident, has no celebrated architecture or hasn't even a well-known derogatory association?

☐ THE questioner could consider Slammanan, near Cumbernauld, in Central Scotland; Harthill, half-way between Edinburgh and Glasgow on the M8; or Whitburn, again

situated on the M8. I am sure at least one of these three would satisfy his criteria.
Greg Russell, Edinburgh.

☐ MELKSHAM, in Wiltshire, must be a strong candidate. Almost all notable houses have long ago been demolished. Its history occupies one slim volume; it tried to be a spa town, emulating Bath, with no success; and it has no famous residents, past or present. I'm quite fond of the place, but what can you say about a town when the talking point for months is the opening of a branch of Sainsbury's?
Pam Thomas, Chippenham, Wilts.

☐ MY NOMINATION: No Man's Land, near Loot, Cornwall. What can there possibly be to say about that place?
Richard Webber, Bristol.

☐ A RAILWAY bridge over the main road into Oldham welcomes you to 'The home of the tubular bandage'. They must be struggling to get into any of the questioner's categories.
Paul Cruthers, Chorlton-cum-Hardy, Manchester.

☐ IN RESPONSE to Pam Thomas, Melksham is recorded in the Domesday Book, 1086. When it was a village, the early kings of England used to hunt in what was a forest, which ran from Chippenham to Calne in the north and Semington to Rowde in the south. We can boast we still have 'The Kings Arms Hotel' where in the early 19th century the stage coaches stopped en route from London to Bristol and where they changed horses. Rachel Fowler – sister to John Fowler, who invented the steam plough and revolutionised the cultivation of heavy soil – was a great benefactor to the town. The beautiful parish church, St Michael and All Angels, is about 900 years old, and in the churchyard a 700-year-old yew tree still stands. We can claim two Roundhouses in the town – one

in Church Street dates from the 17th century. Surely it must
be agreed we have some history?
Sheila Wilkinson, Mayor of Melksham, Wilts.

☐ MELKSHAM, as named by Pam Thomas, is famed as the
birthplace of the Quaker naturalist Dr John Rutty, whose
name is perpetuated throughout Africa by handsome shrubs
called Ruttya. He was the author of *An Essay Towards the
Natural History of the County of Dublin* published in 1772,
of a work on mineral waters of Ireland and, most famously,
of an extraordinary *Spiritual Diary* published posthumously.
Charles Nelson, Wisbech, Cambs.

☐ GREG Russell is wrong. Slammanan, Harthill and
Whitburn have all been mentioned in a national newspaper.
Lawrence Cairns-Smith, Kings Norton, Birmingham.

☐ LORD Horne (of Slammanan) adopted his title after a
political career as a Tory politician during the inter-war period
and a cabinet officer during the General Strike, also accruing
various other honours. I can, however, vouch for the blandness
of the two other towns!
C. Imrie, Balham, London.

☐ YOUR correspondent, Mr Cruthers, is too dismissive.
Oldham was the greatest cotton-spinning town in the world.
The test-tube baby research by Dr Steptoe and his colleagues
was done in Oldham and the first test-tube baby, Louise
Brown, was born there. Among other natives of Oldham are
Sir William Walton and Dame Eva Turner, Eric Sykes, Dora
Bryan and the recent captains of England at cricket and
football, Mike Atherton and David Platt. Sir Winston
Churchill won his first parliamentary seat in Oldham, and
the first Yates Wine Lodge opened in the town.
Alan Myers, Hitchin, Herts.

☐ IF THE search is extended to Ireland, there are numerous examples. Craigavon (Co. Armagh) is famous only for its roundabouts. Strabane (Co. Tyrone) has a tourist information centre, but no tourist attractions. Even its famous ex-sons don't actually come from the town itself, but a few miles up the road. And for years, Letterkenny's sole claim to fame was having the only set of traffic lights in the whole of Co. Donegal. Now the town has two sets, even this claim has evaporated.
Nick Brown, Belfast.

☐ YES. Somewhere in the borders between England and Wales (or is it Scotland?) there is a small village whose name I forget at the moment.
Steve Ellison, Walsall Wood, West Midlands.

QUESTION: My mother died recently at 103 years. Her earliest memory was of 1899, watching Queen Victoria passing by in a horse-drawn carriage. Is there now anyone left alive who can claim to have seen Queen Victoria?

☐ MY MOTHER is aged 104 years and recalls watching Queen Victoria passing by in a horse-drawn carriage during her visit to Bristol in November 1899.
Arthur Bennett, Bristol.

☐ MY GRANDMOTHER, Mrs Minnie Wharnsby, is approaching her 109th birthday, and remembers seeing Queen Victoria, in her carriage, in about 1893. According to a recent interview with the *Basildon Evening Echo*, she was so close that she tried to reach out to the Queen through the carriage window. Having lived all her life in the East End of London, or in Rayleigh, she may well be the oldest Essex girl ever.
Christine Warbis, Cornforth, Durham.

☐ WHEN she was about five years old my future aunt, Madeleine Swale (born 1893) was staying with her family in Finsbury Park, north London. Her elder sister told her that the Queen would be passing the end of the road and suggested they went out together to watch. My aunt said no, she would rather stay indoors and play with her dolls. She's surely the oldest living person to have had the chance to see Queen Victoria and declined to do so?
Alan Swale, Lescure-Jaoul, France.

☐ MY GRANDMOTHER was born in New Zealand in 1892 and first travelled to England in 1899. She recalls watching Queen Victoria – whom she describes as 'a little lady all in black' – pass by in a carriage.
Stephen Goggs, Curtin, Australia.

☐ CHRISTINE Warbis speculates that her grandmother 'may well be the oldest Essex girl ever'. On a stone tablet in the graveyard of St Clement's Church, Leigh, are the words: 'Here lies the body of Mary Ellis . . . She died on the 3rd of June 1609 aged one hundred and nineteen.' On this evidence, there's a little while to go yet!
G. Hemingway, Leigh-on-Sea, Essex.

QUESTION: Where was the original 'Skid Row'?

☐ SKID Row derives from the original Skid Road in Seattle. In 1852, when the settlers moved to a site on Elliott Bay, the local Indians, led by Chief Sealth (hence Seattle), offered free land to a sawmill owner named Henry Yesler. Yesler set up his mill on the waterfront and started work levelling the forests on the surrounding hills. He built a skid for the pioneers (and ox-teams) to roll logs down the steep hill to his mill. The area developed and became associated with the first beerhouse, followed by cheap hotels, bawdy houses and wino

havens – generally an area where nice people did not go! The skid road became Mill Street and today is Yesler Way in the Pioneer Square district of downtown Seattle.
Jack Griffiths, Worthing, W. Sussex.

□ I SAW this expression in Chaucer's *The Man of Law's Tale.*

> He brought her back to Rome, and to his wife
> He gave her, with her little son, and so
> Safe at the Senator's she lived her life.
> Thus could Our Lady lift her out of woe
> As she lifts many from Skid Row.

This dates the expression between 1385–1400.
Katherine Waudby, Derbyshire.

□ EITHER Katherine Waudby's memory is playing tricks on her, or she has been misinformed. The original version of Chaucer's *The Man of Law's Tale*, part three, lines 974–8, reads:

> He bryngeth hire to Rome, and to his whf
> He yaf hire, and hir yonge sone also;
> And with the senatour she ladde hir yf.
> Thus kan oure lady bryngen out of wo
> Woful Custance and many another mo.

Katherine Waudby's version is the Neville Coghill translation of 1951 with one crucial difference:

> Thus could Our Lady lift her out of woe
> As she lifts many another here below.

William Leece, Garston, Liverpool.

QUESTION: What is the geological explanation for the red rock stacks in Monument Valley, Arizona?

□ THE large sandstone blocks which can reach a height of up to 300 metres are locally known as Buttes and Mesas and are geological features which began to form some 250 million years ago in Permian times. They are a record of deposition, compression, uplifting and erosion. Originally the sandstones and underlying shales were probably deposited in a shallow sea which subsequently dried up as the bed began to rise upwards. Continual aeolian (wind-born) deposition formed a desert of huge sand dunes similar to those found in the present-day Namib, Sahara and Arabian deserts. After an estimated period of 50 million years, the sea once again encroached on the desert and deposited shales, conglomerates and sandstones over the dunes. This deposition, plus the sheer weight of sand, compressed the dunes to form hard sandstone. The red colour is a result of the oxidation of iron minerals within rock. Approximately 70 million years ago, in late Cretaceous times, the area was subjected to further uplifting which formed a broad, elongated dome across the region. This process put great stresses on the massive sandstone beds and left them criss-crossed with faults and fractures. The action of running water, intense winds and continual freeze-thaw opened up these stresses and helped erode the rock; the softer shales and mudstones were easily removed, leaving the hard, more resistant sandstone blocks intact.

Paul Worrall, Rundu, Namibia.

QUESTION: How creative were our forebears in celebrating the first millennium? Did they leave any monuments to it?

☐ THE year 1000 did not produce much excitement and there seems to have been virtually no expectation of an end to the world. The mass of the peasantry would have been unaware of it and the country priesthood, singularly ignorant and uninstructed, probably failed to inform them. Such an abstract milestone was far less important than good harvests and the cycle of the seasons. Even amongst the tiny intelligentsia – the senior clergy and monks – there seems to have been little interest. The chronicler Rodulfus Glaber (the name translates as Ralph the Bald) was keenly aware of the two millennia of 1000 and 1033 but he only suggests that they were occasions of divine grace – wasted on a world which quickly returned to sin. But by about the year 1000, the world *was* changing. The economy was expanding, money coming into circulation and new ideas were circulating. As 1033 approached, huge crowds of people, now having the wherewithal, went to Jerusalem, and Glaber says that a few thought this might portend the coming of an anti-Christ, but makes clear that he was not amongst them. In a curious way the period *has* left its monuments. There was a new mass religious devotion, which combined with the new wealth in the building of 'a white mantle of churches' all over Europe. The great cathedrals are a lasting monument to the vigour and enthusiasm which pervaded Western civilisation around the year 1000.

Dr John France, History Department, University of Wales, Swansea.

☐ IN SUPPORT of Dr France's view that little notice was taken of the first millennium is the fact that few people would have thought of the year in terms of counting from the birth of Christ. The system, invented by Dionysius Exiguus in the sixth century, was used by Bede in the eighth, gradually adopted over the next three centuries and only in the 1050s used consistently by the papacy. Because of Bede, the system was adopted by the compilers of the *Anglo-Saxon Chronicle*, in which the entry for the year 1000 revealed a mundane approach to the subject.

Professor Eric Fernie, Courtauld Institute of Art, University of London.

QUESTION: Which advert first used the expression 'you know it makes sense'?

☐ IT WAS Barbara Castle while Minister of Transport in the late 1960s, trying to convince us of the wisdom of a 50 mph speed limit, I believe in response to an oil crisis.
David Francis, Portsmouth.

☐ DAVID Francis is not correct about the origins. The Labour Party, led by Harold Wilson, narrowly won the October 1964 general election with the slogan 'Let's go with Labour'. In March 1966 he went to the country in an attempt to improve Labour's majority. The slogan on this occasion was 'Vote Labour, you know it makes sense!', and the result was a Labour landslide! The 50 mph speed limit to which Mr Francis refers was introduced as a consequence of the Yom Kippur War and the accompanying 'oil crisis' of 1973–4.
John Gazder, Sunbury-on-Thames, Middlesex.

QUESTION: Any possible solutions to the Mad Hatter's conundrum: 'Why is a raven like a writing-desk?'

☐ LEWIS Carroll himself proposed an answer in the 1897 final revision of *Alice's Adventures*. 'Because it can produce a few notes, though they are very flat; and it is never put with the wrong end in front!' The early issues of the revision spell 'never' as 'nevar', i.e. 'raven' with the wrong end in front. Martin Gardner, in *More Annotated Alice* (1990) gave two possible answers, sent in by readers: 'both have quills dipped in ink' and 'because it slopes with a flap'. In 1991, the *Spectator* held a competition for new answers; among the prize winners were: 'because one has flapping fits and the other fitting flaps'; 'because one is good for writing books and the other better for biting rooks'; and

'because a writing desk is a rest for pens and a raven is a pest for wrens'.
Dr Selwyn Goodacre, Editor, Journal of the Lewis Carroll Society, *Swadlincote, Derbys.*

QUESTION: By percentage, which mass-produced consumer item shows the greatest difference between cost of manufacture and sale price?

☐ FORGED £50 notes.
Bill Hirst, Chester.

☐ TELEPHONE calls. They cost nothing to make yet BT charges us a fortune for the privilege.
Frank J. Hollis, Welwyn Gdn City.

☐ GREETINGS cards – two to three pounds for a small rectangle of thin card with colour printing on a quarter of it. Even more unacceptable when the printing is a picture of cuddly teddy bears.
Nigel Allinson, Manchester.

☐ WATER costs nothing to manufacture, it falls from the sky as rain and may be collected and used by anyone without further processing, therefore the percentage difference between cost and sale price is infinite, whatever the sale price. Payment for water covers the cost of removal or neutralisation of contaminants introduced after production (e.g. filtration, chlorination), storage and transport costs (reservoirs and pipelines) and water company profits.
Colin Moretti, Sunbury-on-Thames, Middx.

☐ How about children's bubble bath? Sainsbury's SavaCentre sells a children's brand which is 10 times the price per unit of its basic adult bubble bath. Assuming the adult product

makes a worthwhile margin, the return on the children's product must be extraordinary.
Kieran Daly, Kingston-upon-Thames, Surrey.

☐ A SINGLE cigarette. Cost of manufacture – probably less than one penny. You pay for it with your life.
Matthew Payne, Hampton, Middx.

☐ THE *Pentagon Catalog* by Christopher Cerf and Henry Beard (Workman Publishing Company, 1986), details the findings of various US Senate Committees on the bargains available from defence contractors supplying the US military. These include: a small steel pin (antenna motor assembly alignment pin) $7,417 (mark-up approximately 15,000 per cent); a small steel nut, $2,043 (15,000 per cent); a small allen key (antenna hexagonal wrench) $9,609 (80,000 per cent). Perhaps our own defence industry can provide similar examples.
Mike Evers, Horwich, Lancs.

☐ IN MY local, a pint of lemonade costs £1.72. In a shop, I can buy a litre of lemonade for 30p, therefore the soft drinks are marked up by about 1500 per cent.
Copland Smith, Chorlton-cum-Hardy, Manchester.

☐ A DAMIEN Hirst spot painting of the 'mass produced' 6ft × 8ft variety costs around £600 to make (inclusive of assistant's labour). The current selling price of £25,000 represents a 4,167 per cent increase. A pizza (often held up as one of the best cost-to-profit items, and which, coincidentally, resembles a Hirst 'spin painting') can, even when sold in the most expensive restaurants, only manage a 1,000 per cent increase.
P. Britten, Islington, London N1.

☐ CDS (of the music variety) apparently cost about £1 to produce, but generally sell for over £13. A record company

manager was reported as saying that they would not sell more if the price were lower, but he obviously hadn't heard of market forces. More annoying (for an addict), however, is the price of potato crisps. The production costs of the contents can hardly exceed 0.3p, with a sale price of 15 to 35p. Presumably the packaging makes up the price.
Neil Tozer, Bad Kreuznach, Germany.

QUESTION: Are there any names that I am not allowed to use if I want to change my name by deed poll?

YOU can't change your name by deed poll (or by statutory declaration, which is cheaper), whatever your solicitor and others may lead you to believe. In law your name is what you are known by (legitimately including aliases – for example, pen names, stage names, women using both married and maiden names). A deed poll is only a formal declaration of intent, but it has no relevance if you use a different name in practice. Say your name is John Smith. You go into a solicitor's office and execute a deed poll 'changing' your name to Elvis Presley (it's happened). If, on coming out of the office, you continue to sign your cheques 'John Smith', your name is still 'John Smith'; if you start signing them 'Cliff Richard' then your name is Cliff Richard. Of course, you need to be consistent, and the bank and the Inland Revenue will require evidence that you really are the person known as what you say you are (which is why deeds poll are taken, for practical purposes, as 'evidence'). There is no legal restriction on the name you are known by, but the *use* of that name is subject to all the obvious restrictions on the use of language generally: obscenity, fraudulent impersonation, electoral malpractice, racism, blasphemy, libel and slander. So you can call yourself 'Her Majesty the Queen' as long as you don't pretend to be the Queen. You could *probably* get away with calling yourself Coca-Cola (after all, you can't really be

prevented from calling yourself W. H. Smith, F. W. Woolworth or Ronald McDonald) provided that you didn't do it by way of trade or affecting anyone else's, although I wouldn't vouch for the behaviour of courts in the United States.
Dr J. B. Post, Axbridge, Somerset.

☐ A FEW years ago I read of a man who wanted to change his name to his favourite chatline number. However, his bank refused to accept it as a signature for his cheque book on the basis that it was too easily forged.
Mark Wilkinson, Uxbridge, Middx.

QUESTION: What is the minimum size for Noah's Ark on the basis of two of every known species and enough food for six weeks (assuming the animals wouldn't eat each other)?

☐ THE size of Noah's Ark is immutable, for God said (Genesis 6:15) it had to be 300 cubits long, 50 cubits wide and 30 cubits high (450ft by 75ft by 45ft). If the questioner wants to know what size an Ark would have to be to fit the conditions laid down in the Bible, then this is completely different. Noah was told to take into the Ark seven of each clean beast, seven of each fowl of the air and two of each unclean beast. They were in the Ark for over 12 months, not six weeks. The animals would have to eat one another, for carnivores cannot live off hay. So to survive, not only would space be needed for the animals that were to be saved but also for animals to be used as food. There would also have to be space to store many, many tons of widely varying foodstuffs for them all. There would have to be space to store thousands of boxes in which to keep insects to feed to the insect eaters that were being saved. There would have to be space to grow plants for the pollen, fruit and nut eaters. Space would be needed for gallons upon gallons of fresh water. Also tanks for

freshwater fish and sea fish for feeding to the fish eaters. And, of course, space would be needed for exercising. There would have to be space for thousands of tons of fodder and animals to support them all when the deluge ended. Then there would also have to be space in the Ark to store millions of seeds, seedlings and cuttings for them to re-plant the world, for 'every living substance was destroyed' (Genesis 7:23). How big the Ark, then? The size of the Isle of Wight?
R. Lord, Bolton, Lancashire.

□ I ASSUME this correspondence is closed, now that we have had the definitive answer from R. Lord.
Steve Babbage, Newbury, Berks.

QUESTION: What is the origin of 'kick the bucket'?

□ MOST etymologists agree that the 'bucket' refers to a kind of yoke that was used to hold pigs by their heels so that they could be slaughtered, and was particularly used in parts of Norfolk. The subsequent death-throe spasms of the unfortunate animals created the impression that they were 'kicking the bucket'. The derivation is either from Old French *buquet* – 'a balance' – or the fact that the raising of the yoke on a pulley resembled a bucket being lifted from a well. The term is known to date from at least the 16th century. The more interesting (and probably apocryphal) origin relates to suicides who would stand on a large bucket with noose around the neck and, at the moment of their choosing, would kick away the bucket.
Andy Parkin, Moortown, Leeds.

□ MANY modern American English words – most notably 'jazz' and 'OK' – owe their origins to African languages, dialects and word formations. Originally popularised by

black-face minstrels, 'Kick the bucket' comes, via *kickeraboo* (dead), from the West African Ga words *kekre* (stiff) and *bo* (to end up), and also the Sierra Leone Creole Krio *kekerabu* (dead).
Tony Aitman, Black Voices, Liverpool.

☐ DURING the late 1880s, the American saloon bar was no more than a retreat for the alcoholics of these developing towns (much the same as it is now, one would guess). During this period the use of spit buckets was widespread. The buckets commonly used by drinkers contained the phlegm produced by chewing tobacco. According to '*Developing America – Winning the West and Losing the South*' by Ray Shortland (Farrago Press: 1974) the phrase derived from the death of a famous saloon owner. Joe Dempsy, an Irish immigrant, ran a small bar in Happylanding, Mississippi. Plagued by ill-health due to excess drinking, the story goes that while he was sharing a drink with friends at a table in the bar he collapsed from liver failure; falling from his stool, his feet disturbed the spit bucket. Assuming the collapse was due to drunkenness his drinking partners exclaimed 'he's kicked the bucket'. This phrase was deemed terribly amusing due to the unpleasantries it contained. When later it was realised that Dempsy had died the manner of his death developed into this saying. Shortland attributes the wide use of the phrase to the human condition of refusing to talk openly about death. 'The phrase spread quickly as Happylanding was a port and many traders would drink at the saloon.' It remains to be told whether the contents of the bucket were ever cleaned up.
Adam Cumiskey, West Molesey, Surrey.

☐ TONY Aitman must be disabused as to the African origin of the word 'jazz'. It is of a distinctly dubious etymology; occasionally one comes across suggestions that it derives from 'jass' – supposedly a slang expression for sexual intercourse.

But there are many other theories: from the French verb *jaser* – to chatter; from 'chasse beau' alleged to be a Louisiana dance figure; and that jazz is a corruption of the Cajun slang expression for a prostitute, *Jezabel* – pronounced as 'jasse-belle'. But jazz was not a word often employed by early New Orleans musicians themselves (as an examination of the hundreds of musicians' cards in the New Orleans Jazz Museum reveals).
Brian Wood, Walmer, Kent.

QUESTION: Where in the British Isles do you find the highest density of public houses?

☐ I ALWAYS understood that it was Newton Stewart in Galloway, south-west Scotland.
Alan Stewart, Chelnsley Wood, Birmingham.

☐ WARRINGTON, Cheshire, boasts at least 37 pubs all within half a mile of the town centre. Not a small contributory factor to my current address. During the 1950s, there were many more, due mainly to its two local breweries and the stationing of the Army, Navy, Air Force and the US Air Force in the town.
Michael Gartland, H. M. Prison Wynot, Preston, Lancs.

☐ PERHAPS of equal interest is that the *lowest* density is to be found in Southend-on-Sea, Essex. This is due to the local influence of the Salvation Army.
Peter Turnbull, Leeds.

☐ IN THE area of Norwich bounded by the inner ring road – about 1 mile in diameter centred on the castle – there are about 50 pubs, giving a density of about 1 pub per 10 acres.
Tony Meacock, Norwich.

QUESTION: What is the ultimate irony?

☐ THE one after the penultimate one.
Dave Hewitt, Glasgow.

☐ 'THAT we see death every day and yet live our lives as if we were immortal' (*The Mahabharata*).
David Cottis, Putney, London.

☐ THAT it takes a lifetime to uncover the purpose of one's existence and by then it's too late to benefit from the knowledge.
S. R. Holland, Manchester.

☐ SURELY the presentation of the Nobel Peace Prize to Henry Kissinger.
Kenneth Woodward, Wrexham, Clwyd.

☐ THE second law of thermodynamics (simply stated, heat flows from hot to cold) predicts that the universe will reach a final state of thermodynamic equilibrium, or maximum entropy, at which time the universe will be dead. Indeed, if the universe has any purpose, it must end, for to continue after reaching that purpose would be pointless. The ultimate irony is that the universe dies to make a point.
James Baird, Woodstock, Georgia, USA.

☐ SORRY to disappoint James Baird, but the universe is not going to die. The second law of thermodynamics applies only to closed systems, which the necessarily infinite universe is not. The ultimate irony is that advanced scientific intelligences are trying to kill off the universe which has given them birth.
Philip Lloyd Lewis, Bournemouth.

☐ PHILIP Lloyd Lewis seems to know something that cosmologists don't when he says that the universe is not going to die. The question dominating cosmology is whether the universe is 'open', expanding for ever, or 'closed', contracting to destruction in a 'big crunch'. It depends on how much invisible 'dark matter' there is and whether its gravitational attraction can reverse the expansion of the universe. The ultimate irony would be for scientists in the remote future to conclude that the universe is open and therefore will last for ever and be interrupted in their deliberations by the Big Crunch. Mr Lloyd Lewis says that the universe is necessarily infinite. Again, he is being definite about a contentious scientific debate. The best way to describe the universe is to think of it as an expanding sphere with the planets, stars, galaxies and everything on the surface. It has no boundaries, but is still finite.
Peter Stockill, Berwick Hills, Middlesbrough.

QUESTION: Apart from 'Summer Holiday', which is the worst song ever recorded?

☐ 'TIPTOE Through the Tulips', performed in ghastly falsetto by the unlamented Tiny Tim.
David Lewis, Prevessin-Moens, France.

☐ IT HAS to be 'Mouldy Old Dough' by Lieutenant Pigeon. These seventies misfits were so far removed from pop performers of the day that they even had one of the band's mother on keyboards!
Norman Morrison, Peterborough.

☐ I REMEMBER a Kenny Everett radio programme several years ago which invited listeners to vote for the worst record ever. 'Long-Haired Lover From Liverpool' by Little Jimmy Osmond was beaten into second place by 'The Shifting

Whispering Sands' sung, or rather intuned, by Eamon Andrews. If there is a worse song I hope I don't hear it.
Brian Gunn, Sompting, W. Sussex.

☐ 'THIS Pullover' by Jess Conrad would be my nomination. 'This pullover that you gave to me/ I am wearing and wear it constantly./ Soft and warming like your love for me/ it was made, dear, like you were made for me', and so on . . . At the same time surely anything penned by Ringo Starr deserves mention.
Dave Hastings, Wood Green, London N22.

☐ 'FAIRYTALE of New York' by the Pogues and Kirsty MacColl, which features the memorable lines: 'You scumbag/ you maggot/you lousy old faggot/Happy Christmas my arse/ I hope this is our last.'
Bob Heys, Ripponden, Halifax.

☐ 'FIND Mister Zebedee! *Kind* Mister Zebedee! *Here's* where he said he'd be . . .' followed by some guff about caring schoolkids searching for their retiring teacher so they can present him with a token of their esteem – all sung in the style of a herd of elephants on happy pills. It was played *ad nauseam* on Radio Luxembourg around 1971.
Chris Davies, Ilford, Essex.

☐ WHEN we couldn't get a seat in the pub, we used to play 'O Superman' by Laurie Anderson on the jukebox. It worked every time. The runner-up has to be 'Lucky Star' by Dean Friedman.
A. James, Powys.

☐ ACCORDING to Aldous Huxley it must be 'Mammy', as sung by Al Jolson in *The Jazz Singer* movie of 1927. Huxley said: 'My flesh crept as the loudspeaker poured out those sodden words, that greasy sagging melody. I felt ashamed of myself

for listening to such things, for even being a member of the species to which such things are addressed.'
R. Allem, Chevington, Suffolk.

☐ I OWN a copy of the original tape from Kenny Everett's 1978 World Worst Record show, when the Top Five was as follows: (1) 'I want my baby back' – Jimmy Cross; (2) 'Wunderbar' – Zarah Leander; (3) 'Paralysed' – The Legendary Stardust Cowboy; (4) 'The Shifting Whispering Sands' – Eamonn Andrews; (5) 'Transfusion' – Nervous Norvus.
Maria Monks, Doncaster.

☐ 'TIPTOE Through the Tulips' is not really such a bad song; it is only that the squawking, freakish, Tiny Tim ruined it as he would any number he attempted. When sung in the music halls, it came over quite pleasantly. The worst songs are those without a decent tune, coupled with banal words – as almost any 'musical' in the West End will testify.
Terry Mullins, London N7.

QUESTION: A GOOGOL is 10^{100} (1 followed by 100 zeros). Can there possibly be a googol of anything in the universe?

☐ *MATHEMATICS and the Imagination* by Edward Kasner and James Newman (Bell & Sons, 1949) states that, although the total number of electrons in the universe (10 to the power of 79) is less than a googol, the total possible moves in a game of chess (10 to the power of 10 to the power of 50) is considerably larger than a googol. The book claims the name 'googol' was invented by Kasner's nephew at the age of nine. He also named an even larger number, the googolplex, which is one followed by a googol zeros.
Bill Lythgoe, Wigan.

☐ PHYSICIST David Bohn, in *Wholeness and the Implicate Order*, suggests that there may be 1089 universes existing simultaneously – or maybe more. So we may be in only one of a googol of universes.
Christopher Lee, Shrawley, Worcester.

☐ IF WE take a conservative estimate based on quasar observations that the universe has a diameter of 13 billion light years and then we apply one of the smallest units of measure, the Angstrom, we come up with the fascinating result that the volume of the observable universe equals 2.4 million google cubic Angstroms.
Andy Parkin, Leeds.

QUESTION: What is the most commonly believed untruth?

☐ EITHER 'There is a God' or 'There is not a God'.
Robert Evans, Great Sutton, Cheshire.

☐ THAT this is a free country, and that those who are innocent will have nothing to fear.
Dougie Firth, London SW9.

☐ THERE are three: 'Your cheque is in the post'; 'Of course I love you, darling'; and 'I'm the man from the ministry and I am here to help you'.
Terry Philpot, Oxted, Surrey.

☐ THAT men are sentient beings.
Michelle Varney, Nottingham.

☐ THAT beliefs can be divided into truths and untruths.
Kevin Tweedy, London SE13.

☐ 'THERE'S another bus right behind'; or 'There's nobody else – I just need some space.'
William Barrett, London NW10.

☐ THAT the word 'truth' has anything to do with the idea of fact. 'Truth' is a word with an Anglo-Saxon root, 'treow', that has to do with belief, not fact. 'There is a god' and 'There is not a god' are each true statements, for some people. And beliefs aren't untruths at all! The Latin counterpart to our word 'truth' is *'fides'*, which is faith.
Bert Hornback, Louisville, Kentucky, USA.

☐ BERT Hornback illustrates the second most commonly believed untruth: that what a word once meant is what it continues to mean for ever. The Anglo-Saxon root from which 'truth' is descended is irrelevant. The word from which 'treacle' descended meant a medicine, rather than a syrup; so what? If Hornback is right we ought to reject 'candidates' who are not robed in white; and not call his belief 'silly' because there is nothing holy about it . . .
John Levitt, Leek, Staffs.

☐ IN THIS country, it must be that the greatest playwright and poet was a man who lived in Stratford upon Avon in the 16th century. Intensive research over 250 years has failed to produce a single fact which proves conclusively that Shakspere was the writer William Shake-speare. Shakspere never claimed to be an author of any kind, his death went unnoticed by literary London and for generations after his death there was no recognition of him in Stratford, not even amongst his own family, as anything other than a property and grain merchant. We simply do not know who was 'William Shake-speare'. Many serious scholars have studied what the records do tell us of the Stratford man, and have concluded that he was not the author. The truth is that an authorship problem does exist but the literary establishment refuses to recognise

this fact. Until it does and serious research is devoted to finding the true author, children will continue to be told the Stratford fairy story.
Brian Hicks, Cambridge.

☐ I MUST take issue with Brian Hicks. I think it was Dr Johnson who said that if the plays and sonnets were not written by William Shakespeare, then it must have been another man with the same name. There is plenty of evidence not only that the writer came from Stratford and put on the plays that are attributed to him; but also that he became immensely rich from so doing and retired back to Stratford where he bought the finest house in town. The vanity of writers is such that we may be sure that had anyone else written such good stuff they would have been quick to attach their name to it. The answer to the question of the most commonly believed untruth is, of course, conspiracy theories – Oswald didn't shoot Kennedy, aliens have landed, Elvis lives, etc. That someone else wrote Shakespeare is merely an early example of such.
Ralph Lloyd-Jones, London SE24.

☐ CONTRARY to Ralph Lloyd-Jones's opinion, there is as far as I know no direct evidence that the Stratford 'Shakespeare' ever wrote anything other than his own name, but lots of evidence that he is unlikely to have been the real Shakespeare. First, there are six surviving signatures, all to legal documents. These are abbreviated, all are spelled 'Shaks . . .'. There is no other surviving handwriting. There are no manuscripts of plays or poems, and no letters. Second, none of the Stratford man's family, down to his grand-daughter's death in 1670, nor anyone else in Stratford at that time, has left any mention that he was a famous playwright. He is only once reliably quoted, and then on a matter of land enclosure. The 'Stratford Story' has only really been established 'truth' since David Garrick took it up in 1769 – 153 years after its 'hero'

died. And third, in the burial register this man is baldly
described as 'Will Shakspere gent'. The famous Stratford
monument was installed around 1620, but in 1748 or before
was revamped to change the bust of the dead man and
introduce the quill pen and sheet of paper in his hands –
before then engravings show both hands clasping a sack.
C. A. Banks, Catford, London.

☐ C. A. BANKS should do some reading. The extant number
of Shakespearean signatures is put at eight or nine by
Schoenbaum and Gary Taylor. The spelling of the Stratford
playwright's name has indeed changed, but as a result of our
standardising of spelling, not there being different men of
similar name. Moreover, the play *Sir Thomas More*, by all
reasonable standards, includes some lines in Shakespeare's
hand, preserved for us in the manuscript.
D. G. Banks, Edinburgh.

☐ THE theory that Shakespeare was not known as a playwright in his native town has to contend with two awkward
facts. Firstly, the vicar of Stratford, 50 years after his death,
was purveying a story of his drunken carousing with Ben
Jonson; and secondly, that in his will, dictated in the town, he
left money to 'my fellowes, John Hemmings, Richard Burbage
and Henry Cundell . . . to buy them ringes'. If he was not a
playwright, just how did he come to be on such intimate
terms with so many prominent figures on the London theatre
scene?
Cyril Aydon, Banbury, Oxon.

☐ REGARDING the question of Shakespeare's monument in
Holy Trinity Church, Stratford-upon-Avon: it is true that in
Dugdale's *Antiquities of Warwickshire* published in the
early 17th century, the engraving of the Shakespeare bust
shows a figure with the hands resting on a cushion and not
holding a pen. The monument as it exists has the hands on

the cushion but holding a pen, thus symbolising literary pretensions. The suggestion is that Dugdale's illustration is an accurate representation of the original figure and that the literary references were added later when the bust was restored in the 18th century. Some go further and say (inaccurately) that Dugdale's engraving shows the figure grasping a sack, which was the conventional sign for the profession of maltster, and allege that this shows Shakespeare's actual profession. Unfortunately we cannot take Dugdale's work as accurate. His engravings of monuments from churches across Warwickshire show scores of serious differences from the monuments as they exist – as can be seen by looking at the engravings of other monuments in Holy Trinity, to go no further. We have no reason to believe that his work on the Shakespeare monument is uniquely accurate. I am aware of no other evidence for a major alteration in the form of the Shakespeare monument, and at least one piece of counter-evidence exists; the report of the Master of Stratford School at the time of the repair of the monument, specifically saying that no features were added or removed. Those who try to draw conclusions from the alleged discrepancy are I suggest misleading themselves. Regarding the alleged 50 years' silence of Shakespeare's family on his supposed literary accomplishments, doubters may care to look at the wider history of the times. At the time of Shakespeare's death political passions were stirring which led in the next 40-odd years to civil war, republican revolution and the restoration of the monarchy. Stratford was a Puritan stronghold which in Shakespeare's lifetime banned the performance of plays within the town boundaries. Attitudes to literature were often politically charged. In the immediate aftermath of his death his family in Stratford may well have found it advisable to downplay his literary connections. Shakespeare's descendants appear to have had royalist leanings – Queen Henrietta Maria was a guest of Shakespeare's daughter at New Place at one period of the war. Given

the subsequent Cromwellian interregnum if they did not publicly reflect on their ancestor's accomplishments until well after the restoration of the monarchy in 1660 that wouldn't be surprising. It may indeed not have been safe to do so. My own view is that, contrary to the opinion of conspiracy-seekers, there is ample evidence that the man Shakespeare of Stratford was the same Shakespeare who was a leading actor and impresario in the most renowned theatrical company of the age; and that the actor Shakespeare was accepted by his professional colleagues and other contemporaries as author of the plays bearing his name. Since a resident dramatist would be expected to alter, cut or expand material to order, it would be difficult for an illiterate bumpkin to carry off a long-term deception. We can be surer of Shakespeare's work being his own than of most of the other popular dramatists of the era.
Edis Bevan, Milton Keynes.

☐ SURELY the real point about Shakespeare and the texts is not who did or did not write them, but that they *are written*. They are there to be enjoyed, studied, performed or whatever as great works of literature. In the post-modernist argot, the author *is* dead, long live us readers.
Chris Fagg, Deptford, London SE8.

QUESTION: Is there any single sporting contest longer than the five-day cricket test match?

☐ THE Paris-Dakar rally; the Whitbread Round the World Yacht Race; the Tour de France (Tour of Spain, Tour of Italy); Trans-Australia Ultrathon (a running race across Australia); the dog-sled race across Alaska; any season-long championship (Grand Prix, Football Leagues); any mountaineering expedition (if mountaineering is a sport); Wimbledon (may be counted as a single event for the champion). It

depends on definitions of 'a single contest' but there certainly are many sporting events where the winner must compete for far longer than five days to beat the opposition.
Gareth Yardley, Edinburgh.

☐ I AM told that North American native lacrosse matches used to span a pitch several miles square and continue over the summer. They were often violent contests substituting, at times, for warfare. Maybe modern wars are the longest sport?
James Strapp, Mortlake, London SW14.

☐ IF BOARD games are allowable, then *go* (Japanese name *igo*, Chinese *weiqi*, Korean *baduk*), an elegant game of oriental origin involving the placing of black and white 'stones' on a board so as to surround and/or capture the opponent's pieces, easily exceeds this. The time allotted each player in a top-level tournament may be as much as 40 hours, giving a total length, not including overtime, of 80 hours. The 1938 challenge match between the reigning champion Shusai and his challenger, Kitani Minoru, was played over 60 sessions between June and December.
Andrew Ketley, Cheltenham, Glos.

☐ BEFORE the war it was customary for the World Professional Billiards Championship final to be a single match of two weeks' duration, two two-hour sessions a day. The World Snooker final was also of two weeks' duration (best of 145 frames) from 1946 to 1952, but then reverted to a week's match of 73 frames which it remained until 1972. It is now best of 35, spread over two days. In some pre-War test cricket series, the deciding match was supposed to be timeless, but South Africa v. England was still abandoned as a draw after 10 days in 1919 because England had to catch the boat home.
Clive Everton, Snooker Scene, Edgbaston, Birmingham.

☐ IN THE United States, the annual finals in both baseball (World Series) and basketball (NBA Finals) are decided by best-of-seven series, usually spread over about nine days including rest days. Even during the regular season, baseball teams often play series of three or four matches against the same opponents on consecutive days.
Nick Baker, New York, USA.

☐ THE Iditarod is a yearly dog-sled race in Alaska that starts in Anchorage and ends 1,049 miles later in Nome. The fastest winner took nine days and the slowest winner 20 days.
Colin Painter, St Louis, Missouri, USA.

☐ IF NICK Baker's suggestion of the baseball world series is allowed, how about a six-match cricket test series? This normally runs from early June to late August, nearly three months. So cricket wins again.
Richard Carden, Harleston, Norfolk.

☐ CORRESPONDENCE chess. International journeys are scheduled to take several years, and inefficient or disrupted postal communication in difficult parts of the world mean that a month per move is not exceptional. All one needs then is to participate in one of the occasional games of 100 moves plus.
Martyn Smith, Great Barr, Birmingham.

☐ SINCE Martyn Smith has introduced correspondence chess, one should also allow postal fantasy and science fiction games, many of which are designed to offer 'alternative lives' and to run for ever. The longest-running games have been going for 12 years and show no sign of slowing.
Nick Palmer (editor, The Flagship of Postal Gaming), Nuthall, Notts.

QUESTION: What is the origin of the phrase 'back to square one'?

☐ THERE were many board games, popular in the 19th and early 20th centuries, with numbered squares similar to Snakes & Ladders, where a player landing on a square carrying a penalty might have to go 'back to square one' – and this is clearly the origin of the phrase. Despite *Brewer's Dictionary of Phrase and Fable* and other books such as the *Dictionary of Modern Phrase*, the phrase has no connection with radio commentaries on football matches. As a boy in the 1930s, I regularly listened to such broadcasts while following the movement of the ball on a football-pitch chart in the *Radio Times* which was divided into eight squares. Captain H. B. T. Wakelam gave the commentary while Charles Lapworth would murmur 'Square 3' . . . 'Square 5' . . . as the ball moved about the field. Wakelam never mentioned the squares, and Lapworth said nothing else. The phrase 'back to square one' was never used. On the 50th anniversary of broadcast commentaries in 1973, an article in the *Radio Times* credited the phrase to these commentaries, but one has only to look at the diagram to see that the phrase could have no relevance: 'back' to one team would be 'forward' to the other; the restart after a goal was never in square one; and a pass-back to goal could also be 'back to square two', 'square seven' or 'square eight'. *Norman Brindley, Caddington, Beds.*

QUESTION: Who invented the zip fastener, and when?

☐ THE fast slide fastener was patented by Whitcomb L. Judson of Chicago in 1893. This consisted of a series of hooks and eyes that fastened together with a slider. The more modern type of zip, using a meshed tooth arrangement, was patented by Gideon Sundback in 1913. Zip fasteners were

first used in men's trousers and did not appear in women's clothing until the 1920s.
Nick Spokes, Ilford, Essex.

☐ THE zip didn't take off until 1918 when the US Navy realised that it would make an excellent fastener for flying suits. The name zipper was coined in 1926, and has since been shortened to zip in the UK.
Nicola Baxter, Redland, Bristol.

QUESTION: Are there other people who, like the Queen, are heads of state of more than one country?

☐ THE President of France, by the constitution of 1993, is the co-prince and thus joint head of the state of Andorra. The other prince is the Spanish Bishop of Urgel. The President holds this title as the successor to the Count of Foix, the original co-prince when Andorra was established in 1278, via the Bourbon kings of France.
Benjamin Elton, Manchester.

☐ THIS query begs questions on the meaning of the term 'country': one person's sovereign state is another's commonwealth of autonomous entities. Was the former USSR one country or 15? Is Cataluña a country, or a region of Spain? Is Puerto Rico a country ruled by the US?
Barry Stierer, Brighton.

☐ MACAO is still under Portuguese control; and Kurdistan is ruled by five heads of states – Iran, Iraq, Turkey, Russia and Syria. And we must consider the King of Sweden, the President of Finland and the Queen of Denmark: the first for the island of Gotland, with a political structure similar to the Isle of Man's; the second for Aland, Aaland or

Ahvenanmaa; and the third for Greenland and the Faroe Islands.
Jorge Machado, Harrow, Middlesex.

QUESTION: What was the original cock-and-bull story?

☐ IN STONY Stratford, Buckinghamshire (now part of Milton Keynes), there are two old coaching inns on the main road (now the A5) from London to the north, which were the first overnight stop for coaches leaving London and the last stop for coaches travelling to London. Gossip circulated between the bars of these inns in a version of 'Chinese whispers' fuelled by good ale, inevitably ending up completely inaccurate. The inns are called the Cock and the Bull.
Gyan Mathur, Brussels, Belgium.

☐ THE original story is at the end of *The Life and Opinions of Tristram Shandy*, by Laurence Sterne. The bull is apparently unable to sire a calf.
Stephen Maybank, Reading, Berks.

☐ GYAN Mathur's explanation is an excellent example of a cock-and-bull story. *Brewer's Phrase and Fable* says: 'The origin of the term is probably connected with old fables in which cocks, bulls and other animals discoursed in human language. In Bentley's Boyle Lecture (1692) occurs the passage "That cocks and bulls might discourse, and hinds and panthers hold conferences . . ." '
E. S. Webber, Cairns, Queensland, Australia.

QUESTION: Who, when and where was the first recorded case of a conscientious objector?

□ THE first example of a conscientious objector to military conscription to which we can attach a name, place and date is probably the 1700-year-old case of Maximilian. He was from Thevesta, a Roman colony in north Africa. Along with other inhabitants who were Roman citizens he was called up to join the military. When he refused, on the grounds of his Christianity, he was summarily beheaded. This was on the date we would now call 12 March, in AD 295. Maximilian was the earliest we explicitly commemorated when Sir Michael Tippett unveiled Britain's first public memorial to conscientious objectors through the ages, in London's Tavistock Square in 1994.
Albert Beale, Chairperson, Peace Pledge Union, London N7.

□ IT WAS Lysistrata, who organised a mass denial of conjugal comforts by the women of Athens in an effort to get their men to stop the Peloponnesian Wars of the fifth century BC.
Sandy Sanders, Clayton, Victoria, Australia.

QUESTION: I would like to go on 'Mastermind' but I don't have a specialist subject. Which topic of research would give people the impression that I've spent years in a library, whilst consuming the smallest time to master?

□ TRY: (1) yourself; (2) accurate unemployment statistics 1979–1997; (3) the successful war on poverty/drugs/crime/pollution, etc.
Tony Beswick, Tapton, Chesterfield.

□ TRY the Peloponnesian War. There have been many books on the subject, but the sole contemporary source for all

subsequent works is *The History of the Peloponnesian War* by Thucydides. Thucydides did not include anecdotal information, he personally interviewed the protagonists, and excluded anything that could not be checked from another source. It was hundreds of years before other historians took a similarly rigorous approach, and by that time no other contemporary sources from the war were available.
Quentin Langley, Woking, Surrey.

☐ THIS reminds me of a glut of jokes over 30 years ago about the smallest books in the world: e.g. The Very Best of German Humour; Famous Italian War Heroes; 100 Years of Jewish Cricket, etc. I suggest the questioner hunts out one of the following: Men of Probity in the Conservative Party 1979–1997; English Sporting Success Since 1967; The Modernisation of British Rail; Altruism in the Privatised Utilities; The Secret Life of Princess Diana . . .
Richard Handford, Chichester, West Sussex.

QUESTION: Who was or is the Marquis of Granby, and why does he have so many pubs named after him?

☐ JOHN Manners, Marquis of Granby (1721–1770), was commander of the British troops who served under Prince Ferdinand of Brunswick in Germany during the Seven Years' War. He was 'a generous, genial character, much loved by his troops and popular with the public' (Savory, *His Britannic Majesty's Army in Germany During the Seven Years' War*). He was prepared to buy supplies out of his own pocket when official sources failed, and died heavily in debt. A brave fighting soldier, his finest hour was probably when he led Ferdinand's heavy cavalry into action at the Battle of Warburg 31 July 1760), his bald head shining in the sun (hence the phrase 'to charge bald-headed'). As for the pubs, it was common to name them after war heroes (Duke of Wellington,

Nelson, etc.), though their number in this case seems to have been increased by discharged soldiers who set up pubs named after their old commander.
Michael Bell, London SW16.

☐ MICHAEL Bell rightly quotes Savory, that the Marquis of Granby was 'a generous . . . character, much loved by his troops', but misses the main reason why this led to so many pubs being named after him. In the days before pensions for common soldiers or a welfare state, it was established practice for high-ranking officers to buy pubs for men who had served them in some exceptional way. This then acted as a form of pension, and reached a height during and after the Napoleonic War. There was no strict rule as to how or when this honour should be awarded, but the Marquis of Granby was famous for the number of pubs he gave away, and which were named after him in turn. This practice is the main reason for such names in pre-1900 pubs, some of which, such as the Marquis of Lorne in Brixton, south London, may be the only surviving memorial to a lesser (or less generous) leader.
Steve Wilson, London SE2.

☐ MICHAEL Bell gave a very good account of John Manners, Marquis of Granby (1721–70), but the man alluded to in so many public house names is his grandson Samuel Manners (1772–1837). Samuel was an antiquarian with a particular fascination for medieval taverns, many of which were being altered or demolished at the time. He had a couple of the better examples dismantled and rebuilt on his Notting-hamshire estate. Fascination eventually turned to obsession and Samuel even had the façade of the 13th-century 'Saracens Head', Northampton, re-erected as the north wall of his bathroom. Many pubs bearing his name do so in memory of his eccentric passion for public houses, but it is thought that he did pay some landlords to name their pubs after him

during his lifetime, notably the original 'Scruffy Murphy' in Leicester.
Reginald Spandit, The Granby Society, Tewkesbury.

QUESTION: If it were possible for a spaceship to reach the point in the universe where the Big Bang occurred, what would it find there now?

☐ Deaf aliens.
John Ward, Fareham, Hants.

☐ Surely, since the Big Bang occurred a finite time ago, and matter cannot travel infinitely fast, the entire universe must be a sphere of finite diameter, and a sphere has a centre? The location of the centre relative to the Earth could be found if the distance from the Earth to the 'edges' of space can be measured. As light travels faster than matter, a sufficiently sensitive telescope should be able to observe some, if not all, of the universe boundary.
Angelo Valentino, London SW3.

☐ The basis of the Big Bang theory is the so-called Cosmological Principle: that the universe is, roughly speaking, the same at every point in space if observed at the same time. Wherever you went in your spaceship you would therefore see pretty much the same thing as we see around us from Earth. The mistake implicit in the question is to think of the Big Bang as occurring at a point *in* space: the Big Bang creation event represents the origin *of* space. This event was infinitely small and can therefore be regarded as a point, but the point in question contained all of our present Universe (in an infinitely compressed form). There is therefore no need to travel to visit the point where the Big Bang happened. It happened everywhere (including here) but, in the beginning, everywhere was in the same place.

Dr Peter Coles, Astronomy Unit, Queen Mary & Westfield College, London E1.

☐ THE expansion of the universe is more like the three-dimensional equivalent of the surface of a balloon as it is inflated. The single point of the Big Bang has been 'stretched' to form the universe we see today.
Steven Hall, Leigh, Lancs.

☐ ANGELO Valentino's reply would appear to make perfect sense, but although the universe is finite it has no boundary, hence no identifiable centre. In accordance with General Relativity, space curves round on itself like the skin of a balloon. If one were to go on a rocket in a straight line, one would not reach 'the edge' but would, eventually, come back to where one started. As a result of this, the universe must not be thought of as a three-dimensional sphere, but like the three-dimensional surface of a four-dimensional 'hypersphere'. As to 'what happens to the part of the hypersphere underneath the surface?', the answer is, I think, unknown to science.
Donald Baillie, Penicuik, Midlothian.

QUESTION: Will I be celebrating the end of the second millennium on my own on 31 December 2000?

☐ VERY probably. Those of us who are not so stupid as to celebrate it a year too early are mostly also sensible enough to realise that it is not an event worth celebrating at all.
Richard A'Brook, Carnoustie, Angus.

☐ IF WE take into account the fact that in 1752 the month of September had 11 days missing, a more logical position would be to celebrate the end of the millennium on 11 January 2001. Personally I intend to celebrate on 31 December 1999,

31 December 2000 and 11 January 2001; and possibly even on 11 January 2000, just to be safe.
Alan Craig, Shadforth, Durham.

☐ SINCE a millennium is an entirely imaginary unit of time – like all the units of time except the day, the lunar month, and the year – the questioner can celebrate the end whenever he likes. If he wishes to celebrate the end of the second Christian millennium, he should actually have celebrated on 31 December 1995, since Christ was born in 6 BC.
Jane Carnall, Edinburgh.

☐ OBEDIENT French schoolchildren will be celebrating with the questioner. Their textbooks have for long explained that, for example, the second century AD began on 1 January 101 and ended on 31 December 200.
Sir Peter Newsam, Institute of Education, University of London.

☐ THE first day of the Christian era was deemed to be Lady Day AD 1. I shall therefore celebrate the last day of the present millennium on 24 March 2001.
Michael Hudson, Sidcup, Kent.

☐ MICHAEL Hudson might be right to identify Lady Day AD 1 as the first day, but he forgets that in 1752, in the first recorded example of European harmonisation, 11 days were deleted from September; so he needs to pop the cork on 5 April 2001.
Paul Soper.

☐ THE statement, 'Christ was born in 6 BC', is a slur on the scholarly reputation of Dionysius Exiguus, who worked out the year of Christ's birth in the fourth century. The year of Jesus' birth is given in the Gospels by two events which Dionysius could date from Roman official records. Matthew

(2:1) says Jesus was born during the reign of Herod, who died in 749 AUC (4 BC). Luke (2:2) says Jesus was born when Quirinius was Governor of Damascus – he was appointed in 757 AUC (AD 4). Dionysius put the year of Jesus' birth (AD 1) at 753 AUC, which is the best compromise.
Donald Rooum, London SW2.

QUESTION: Why is a cocktail so-called?

☐ THE name originates from one vital component: the decoration. In previous centuries a mixed drink with a spirit base would have been adorned with feathers from the tail of a prize cockerel. Similarly, when a young lady wanted to be the belle of the ball, she would attach the feathers of a cockerel's tail to her dress.
Katheryn Smith, Doncaster, S. Yorks.

QUESTION: When and where did the milk bottle take off in this country? I remember that milk in 1918 was delivered to us by a man with a churn from which he ladled out the liquid into my mother's jug.

☐ MILK bottles took off in Great Britain some time after 1906 when Ernest Lane at the Manor Farm Dairy in East Finchley, north London, pioneered the selling of pasteurised fresh milk in bottles. Previous attempts in 1884, 1887 and 1894 were not so successful. In the US, they were introduced in 1879. It was in 1895 that M. J. Owens produced the first machine to make proper bottles, although the churn method of milk delivery would have continued for many years after their introduction. (Sources: *Robertson's Book of Firsts* and Grimley's *The Origins of Everything*.)
Ivor Solomons, Norwich.

☐ I CAN remember milk being delivered to our Clerkenwell house in a churn as late as the early 1930s. About this time our local dairyman started using wide-necked bottles, sealed with a cardboard disc. The reward for breaking through this was a finger full of delicious cream.
Frank Fletcher, Winchester, Hants.

☐ THE date for milk bottles being generally used is earlier than 1906, stated by Ivor Solomons. My great-grandfather, Dr E. F. Willougby, a general practitioner, was active in promoting improved sanitation throughout this period. A summary of his life, which I believe to be a eulogy at a memorial service held for him following his death in 1906, includes the statement: 'In his advocacy of clean and safe milk, he was the first to suggest the bottling of the public milk supply, which has now become so general.'
Mike Benson, Bedford.

QUESTION: Hierocles is said to have devoted his life to collecting jokes, and to have amassed by his death a grand total of 28. Does anyone have a record of these?

☐ HIEROCLES was one of the authors of a collection of 265 jokes in ancient Greek which has come down to us under the name of *Philogelos* (lover of laughter). Nothing is known of him or his co-author Philagrius, although early printed editions of the collection identified him implausibly with a turgid neoplatonist philosopher of the same name. The story that he devoted a lifetime to collecting just 28 jokes is a modern invention: the first printed edition (1605) was based on a manuscript which happens to contain a selection of 28, concealed between tedious theological tracts. Most of the jokes are of the kind that we would call 'Irish' jokes, but interestingly the butt of most of them is not a racial stereotype but an 'egghead' (*scholastikos*). Their quality varies greatly, but here is one of my favourites: 'An egghead carefully sealed a bottle of vintage wine. But his slave drilled a hole in the bottom and stole some of it. The egghead was amazed that the wine had gone down while the seals were unbroken. Another said: "Maybe it has been taken from the bottom." But the egghead replied: "You idiot, it is not the bottom half that is missing, but the top." It is funnier in Greek. There are also some splendid jokes about people with hernias or bad breath, a much under-researched aspect of Greek civilisation.

Dr J. R. Morgan, Department of Classics and Ancient History, University of Wales, Swansea.

QUESTION: The moon appears to rotate about its own axis in exactly one lunar month; thus we always see the same face of the moon. Why this remarkable co-incidence? Do the moons of other planets behave in the same way?

☐ IN GENERAL, a planet will induce a tidal 'bulge' on a rotating satellite which will induce friction and energy loss, slowing down the rotation until the satellite presents the same face to the planet (synchronous rotation). Because of the moon's elliptical orbit, the presented face does vary a little during orbit. The tidal bulge on the Earth caused by the moon has likewise caused the Earth's rotation to slow down (it appears that 400 million years ago, the day-length was 21.5 hours). In more complex satellite systems, some satellites – although in synchronous rotation – are perturbed gravitationally by other satellites into highly elliptical orbits. Hence, their 'wobble' is greater, which also means that tidal heating is likely to be a major feature. Smaller, irregularly shaped satellites can have a 'chaotic' rotation which is permanent because of the gravitational effect of other satellites.

Brian Daugherty, Open University, Bucks.

QUESTION: Where did the exclamation mark and question mark originate, and why are they practically universal irrespective of the widely differing scripts for various languages?

☐ BOTH these signs were originally manuscript abbreviations in Latin texts. The exclamation mark derives from a vertical version of the Latin word *Io*, meaning 'joy' (the vertical stroke was the I above the o, which eventually became a dot). Similarly, the question mark goes back to the vertically contracted *Q(uaesti)o* (a curly q above the circle/dot). These origins suggest that their prime function was to represent distinctions in intonation; indeed, in some languages the two together can represent incredulity ('You saw a what?!'). Now they are used mainly to give a logical structure to a text. With other textual signs – like the ampersand '&' (a merging of the letters in the Latin word *et*, meaning 'and') – they presumably spread with the languages of the European empires; but native writing systems like Hindi or the Korean Han'gul have not always adopted them.
Peter Sherwood, School of Slavonic and East European Studies, University of London.

QUESTION: The ancestors of dolphins and whales crawled out of the sea, evolved into mammals and then crawled back into the sea. Why did they bother?

☐ BIOLOGY cannot answer the question 'why' because it implies conscious purpose. A more fruitful query would be 'how'. We don't need to confine the argument to whales and dolphins since many orders of mammals and birds have aquatic or partly aquatic members, e.g. beavers, sea otters, seals, hippopotamus, penguins, herons, ducks, gulls and albatrosses. Each of these has the same basic anatomy and physiology as their land-dwelling close relatives, but with a

111

number of adaptations to meet the special demands of their environment. There is no sense in which this can be seen as a 'return' by much earlier life forms. In the case of whales, it is likely that they evolved from carnivorous mammals inhabiting the edges of rivers, lakes and shallow seas some 50 million years ago who, possibly as a result of competition for space and food or pressure from predators, gradually adapted to a fully marine existence. There is very good discussion of the evolution of whales and a review of the fossil evidence of intermediate forms in Stephen Jay Gould's *Dinosaur in a Haystack* (1996).
Michael Hutton, Camberwell, London.

☐ BECAUSE they could. 'Why' questions such as these are usually impossible to answer, as causal theories about evolution cannot be tested and so falsified. All that can be said is that at some stage land-based individuals in a particular circumstance which were able to operate slightly more efficiently in water did better than those which were slightly less efficient. An interesting if scientifically dubious theory, proposed by Sir Alistair Hardy in the thirties, suggested that man's ancestors went down the same line a few million years ago. This, he said, explains a number of interesting human features, most notably our relative baldness and our habit of walking on two legs. Beyond being a neatish story, there is relatively little hard evidence for this 'aquatic ape' theory, and it cannot be tested.
Karl Smith, London SW12.

QUESTION: Prior to the building of the Abbey Wood complex, just north of Bristol, what was the last military establishment in this country to be built surrounded by a protective moat?

☐ FORT Brockhurst at Gosport, Hampshire was built between

1858 and 1862 – one of the so-called Palmerston's Follies – and is now a museum with a splendid moat much enjoyed by the local waterfowl.
J. R. Handford, Gosport, Hants.

QUESTION: Which historical character most influenced history by a decision based on the influence of a woman?

☐ ACCORDING to Lesley Blanch's 1954 book *The Wilder Shores of Love*, Aimée Dubucq de Rivery was captured by pirates as a 16-year-old returning to Martinique from France and given to the Turkish Sultan as a gift. She became the Sultan's favourite wife, and later the mother of his successor. Through her influence with her son, Sultan Mahmoud, she westernised Turkey and vainly attempted to secure France's patronage. But Aimée was also Josephine Bonaparte's cousin, and when Josephine was divorced by Napoleon, mother and son took the news as a personal insult. According to Blanch, they set out, unbeknown to Josephine, to avenge this blot on the family status. Turkey switched allegiances from France to England, signed a treaty with Russia at England's urging, and in so doing sealed Napoleon's eventual defeat against Russia.
Vivienne Kramer, Denver, Colorado, USA.

☐ THIS must surely be when Esther asked King Xerxes to save her people – the Jews, who were all about to be killed by Xerxes' prime minister Haman. She risked her life to do this, but the king granted her request and thus the Jews were saved. Had she not acted there would have been no Jewish race for Christ to have been born into, Christianity might never have existed and world history might have been totally different. See the book of Esther in the Bible for more details!
Jane Simpson, Reading.

QUESTION: Which animal can tolerate the greatest temperature range?

☐ TARDIGRADES or bear animalcules must be among the animals with tolerance to the greatest temperature range. They can be both frozen in liquid nitrogen and boiled under pressure. Aside from this they are also resistant to a variety of corrosive chemicals and can revive after almost complete desiccation. They are able to bear such conditions by entering a state of suspended animation. This they can hold for at least a century.
A. Leask, Sydney, Australia.

QUESTION: What was the cause of the first environment protest in Great Britain? When did it occur?

☐ NED Ludd was a British worker who lived around 1800 and who, in a fit of rage, destroyed supposedly labour-saving machinery belonging to a Leicestershire 'stockinger'. This might have been the first deliberate sabotage against machinery occurring at the time of the Industrial Revolution. Ludd spoke in favour of environmental priorities based on an ethic where industrial growth, regardless of profit, had to be regulated according to such ethical priorities. He was convicted at a mass trial in 1813 for being a 'monkeyrencher', sentenced to death and hanged.
Tim Hope, Bergen, Norway.

QUESTION: Why are people from Newcastle called 'Geordies'?

☐ TECHNICALLY, no inhabitant of Newcastle should be so-called, as the Geordies were the supporters of King George who held the south bank of the Tyne, the area around

Gateshead, while the north bank was held by the Jacobites. It is said that when boats entered the river during the troubles, the sailors would call out to the dockers: 'Are you a Geordie or a Jacobite?' and be directed to the appropriate berth. There are some who still maintain that the only true Geordies are those born between the Tyne and the Wear.
David Sweetman, London E9.

☐ THE origin has been a matter of much discussion, but not a single piece of genuine evidence has ever been produced. After many years trying to find it, the first use of the word I discovered was in 1823. This was by the local comedian, Billy Purvis, who had set up his booth at the Newcastle Races on the Town Moor. When a showman erected his tent nearby, Billy cried out: 'Yor a fair doon reet feul, not an artificial feul like Billy Purvis! Thous a real Geordie!' Clearly in 1823 a Geordie was a fool. In 1788 George III, who was a very unpopular monarch, became insane and although he recovered for a while his son (later George IV) had to be made Regent in 1811 and continued to perform that office until the insane monarch died. George IV was also unpopular – his love of pleasure and his promiscuity were notorious. When he became king in January 1820 he started proceedings to divorce his wife Caroline. The same year there was a huge demonstration in Newcastle in support of her. In the 19th century the middle class of Newcastle disliked and feared the mining community and probably used 'Geordie' as a term of abuse when they referred to pitmen. In England, when the early Hanoverians passed away Geordie gradually ceased to be an insulting word and eventually was accepted as a friendly term when applied not only to pitmen but anyone who lived in this area.
Frank Graham, author, Geordie Dictionary, *Newcastle-upon-Tyne.*

QUESTION: Whence came the Christmas cracker and its fancy hats and silly riddles?

☐ THE origin of the Christmas cracker is attributed to a London baker, Thomas Smith, around 1850. He got the idea, the story goes, from French candies wrapped in coloured paper with the ends twisted together. After adding the chemically treated strip of paper to make the bang, the first crackers he sold contained sugared almonds and a love message. By the early 1900s, Tom Smith's crackers had become so popular worldwide that he opened his own factory and was filling them with all kinds of sweets, novelties, rhymes or jokes.
Frank Abbott, Kyoto, Japan.

QUESTION: A full cooked English breakfast is sometimes referred to as 'The Full Monty'. Why?

☐ IT IS held by some that in the Second World War, Field Marshal Montgomery favoured a comprehensive approach to breakfast and that when the humble squaddies lined up in the morning some of them used to ask for 'the FULL MONTY' rather than just, say, egg and soldiers. Another explanation relates to Montague Burton, a tailor. When customers were asked whether they wanted a two- or three-piece suit, those who wanted a waistcoat said they wanted 'the FULL MONTY'. This also explains why the saying is often used in relation to items other than breakfast.
Roger Williams, Beeston, Notts.

☐ IT WAS once fashionable to decorate one's bumper and radiator with headlights, spotlights, foglights, searchlights and assorted badges to show that one was driving not to work but in the Monte Carlo Rally. An array of this kind was The Full Monte. But there is also a possible connection with the

card game Monte. By winning every trick you collected the whole pack – The Full Monte.
Peter Cordall, Ormskirk, Lancs.

QUESTION: By what criteria can the extent to which a country is civilised be assessed? Which are the most civilised countries?

☐ THIS can be easily determined by whether or not the state practises capital punishment. The degree of civilisation can be measured by the elapsed time since the last execution and by the percentage of the public that is against the return of the death penalty. Thus the UK is now moderately civilised, but precariously so.
Toby Moore, Canberra, Australia.

☐ CIVILISATION derives from the Latin *civis* and *cognates*, meaning citizen and relating to concepts of city-dwelling. So, the criterion by which civilisation could be measured is the extent to which a country's population lives in cities. Thus, Britain would be more civilised than, say, France; and the United States and Japan would probably be amongst the most civilised countries.

Of course, in practice civilisation is really a loaded assessment of moral and cultural superiority, which also derives from European perceptions of classical antiquity and the early Mediterranean city states. It is therefore useless as an objective framework for thinking about societies. A recent trend has been to associate 'civilised' with 'humanitarian', but this is no more helpful, since only wealthy nation states can usually afford to be humanitarian to their neighbours.
J. Dronfield, Cambridge.

☐ IN THE words of Mahatma Gandhi: 'A nation's status of civilisation can be measured by the way it treats its animals.'
Ute Cohen, Las Vegas, Nevada, USA.

☐ I TAKE grave exception to Toby Moore's criterion of the time which has elapsed since the abolition of capital punishment. On this basis Halifax would top this country's barbarity league by reason of, with Hull, staging the last public execution in England. (Hence the expression 'from Hull, Hell and Halifax may the Lord deliver us'). Halifax is now, by virtue of the presence of the building society and Sir Bernard Ingham, arguably the most civilised town in Britain.
Bob Heys, Ripponden, Halifax.

QUESTION: Assuming that most Saxon, Norman and Medieval communities would have required a varied mix of skilled people in order to survive, why are there so many Smiths in relation to Weavers, Coopers, Bakers and Wrights? And what did Jones do originally?

☐ SMITH is from the same root as Smitan which means 'to smite', and is one of the few Old English bynames to be recorded a century before the Norman Conquest. Smith of the 10th century was a worker in iron, smiting ingots into swords, shields, battle-axes, halberds and ploughshares. But the occupational term 'smith' embraced other workers who smote their raw materials; it lost its precision and new names were needed. They were found in another Old English word *wryhta*, 'wright or craftsman', subsequently dividing into Cartwright, Wheelwright, and Wainwright (maker of wains or waggons). With increasing specialisation, a distinction had to be made between a worker in iron and a worker in tin, so more exact definitions were made, hence blacksmith and whitesmith. The smith was an important

man in medieval times, making and repairing swords, lances, defensive iron-works for castles and manor houses, offensive engines for assaulting enemy castles, and peaceful items such as agricultural implements. He was the technologist and technician, the engineer and mechanic of his day. There are several reasons why Smith is such a widespread surname; it is one of the oldest Anglo-Saxon names, so Smiths have been around longer than most. The Smiths of Old England were a strong, lusty, vigorous people capable of raising large families. Smiths were much in demand in medieval and later times; every village had its smithy with one or more smiths working profitably in it, so they and their families are unlikely to have gone hungry in English winters when food was scarce. Because he was not quite so close to the heat of battle in medieval warfare as Archers, Bowman (Bowmen), Knights, and others, Smith probably returned safely to his native village after the war, to resume his work and the care of his family.
Kenneth Allen, Cook, Australia.

☐ SMITHS were very good at picking chastity belts.
Brendan Cooper, Hammersmith, London.

☐ HAVING worked all day on something hot and sweaty, it obviously came naturally to continue at night. I realise that this does not explain the relative lack of Rogers, but I shall leave this to others more expert than I.
Maurice Childs, Bromley, Kent.

☐ THE prevalence of smiths presumably dates from the many centuries when the only mode of transport was a horse. So every town – however insignificant – would have had its own smithy. Perhaps not everyone had a cart (or the wheel rims didn't wear out so fast); so there were not so many wrights, nor much call for barrel-makers (coopers), bakers or weavers. As for Jones, this is a shortened form for Johnson – and

similar abbreviation applies to Evans, Williams, Hughes, Davis, etc.
Graham R. Jones, Withington, Manchester.

☐ IT IS wrong to conclude that there were more smiths than wrights or coopers. Small variations in the frequency of names, which happen by chance, are magnified as the generations pass. I made a computer simulation of a village of 100 couples, with 20 each of Wrights, Smiths, Jones, Coopers and Weavers. I assumed that every couple makes 10 attempts to reproduce, and that each attempt has a 1 in 10 chance of success. This ensures that the population stays roughly stable. The simulation ran for 50 generations (about 1000 years). I tried it 200 times, and the results varied greatly. Usually one or more names die off altogether, and it is very common for one or two names to become dominant. If we could wind back to AD 1100 and start again, the dominant name might turn out to be Weaver or any of the others.
Chris Brew, Edinburgh.

QUESTION: Who was the composer of 'Happy Birthday'?

☐ WORDS and music were by an American nursery teacher called Patty Hill. She wrote it so her children could sing it when someone had a birthday.
Chloe Walker (aged 7), Bristol, Avon.

☐ IT IS, I understand, the world's most sung song. Written in the 1890s, it was not copyrighted until 1935 and is still in copyright. In 1988 the firm which had owned the song since 1935 put it up for sale. This company had been collecting about a million dollars a year in royalties. It was acquired by Warner Communications in a $25 million deal.
Leslie Jerman, Epping, Essex.

QUESTION: What is the origin of the phrase 'to have a chip on one's shoulder'? It sounds American, but where or when?

☐ THIS does seem to be of American origin and derives from a custom once common to bar rooms. A man who felt like a fight put a woodchip on his shoulder and defied anyone to knock it off. The challenge was rarely refused. An Anglo/Irish analogue was (is?) 'trailing the coat'. Here, the would-be gladiator trailed his coat behind him in the hope that someone would tread on it. The formal customs have long ceased but the attitudes remain. Today the allegation that some stranger has merely looked in the wrong direction is deemed sufficient to justify assault. The older usage now seems positively chivalrous.
Alan W. Smith, Chigwell, Essex.

☐ To ANY North American the origin of the phrase 'a chip on one's shoulder' can be a painful memory. My first experience of it, more than 60 years ago, was as an English child in a Canadian playground. The school bully picked a chip of wood from the ground, placed it on his shoulder, and invited me to knock it off. I did so, and was felled by his fist. In time I learnt that the best method of avoiding an unwanted fight, or the taint of cowardice in refusing the challenge, was to place another chip on my own shoulder and dare my opponent (who was sometimes my friend) to knock that off first. This usually succeeded, and the affair ended painlessly in taunting shouts and honours even.
John Prebble, Kingswood, Surrey.

QUESTION: Who was Gordon Bennett?

☐ JAMES Gordon Bennett (1841–1918) was an American journalist, editor of the *New York Herald* (in succession to

his less well-known father, also James Gordon Bennett) and sports enthusiast. He is probably best-known now for being the man who commissioned Henry Morton Stanley to search for Dr Livingstone (thus presumably occasioning a telegram which began 'Gordon Bennett – I've found Livingstone!'). Bennett also introduced polo to the United States and was involved in horse-racing (Leopold Bloom spends some time in *Ulysses* contemplating a bet upon a horse in the Gordon Bennett Handicap, actually run that day in Dublin).
Nicholas Graham, Teddington, Middlesex.

☐ IN JANUARY 1876 Stanley saw a great mountain 'afar off' and named it Mount Gordon Bennett. This was later changed to the Ruwenzori, better known perhaps as the Mountains of the Moon.
Rennie Bere, Bude, Cornwall.

☐ WHEN Bennett opened his newspaper's Paris office in 1887, he was unable to dine at a busy restaurant, so he bought it and sat down to mutton chops.
Paul Crowther, Knutsford, Cheshire.

☐ IN 1900 he donated the Gordon Bennett trophy for a race between national teams of drivers and cars. The complex qualifying process for entry led to the exclamation: Gordon Bennett!
George Hartshorn, Badby, Daventry.

☐ ONCE after a heavy drinking bout at a party arranged by his fiancée, he took advantage of the blazing fire to relieve himself in front of the assembled guests. For which he was thrown out and later horsewhipped by his fiancée's brother with whom he once fought a duel. So as the latest escapade spread among the gossips all shook their heads in disbelief and despair and said, 'Oh, Gordon Bennett!'
Rev. W. Webb, Guildford, Surrey.

☐ MY SISTER-in-law, a born and bred Eastender, insists that 'Gordon Bennett' is just a politely extended form of 'Gawd', to avoid accusations of blasphemy.
Si Cowe, Pickering, N. Yorks.

QUESTION: How did the newt, a graceful and agile creature, come to be regarded as an index of inebriation?

☐ IT WAS a mistake, a mishearing of 'an Ute', as used by US Army personnel in Britain during the Second World War. The celebrated drunkenness of the Ute Indian tribe on their reservation forced the US Government to ban the sale of alcohol there.
Harold Smith, Bradford-on-Avon, Wilts.

☐ THE phrase actually comes down to regional accent in the days of Henry VIII. Half-way through a banquet the king inquired as to what brew one young reveller had been partaking of, to be begged by the young man's father to 'forgive him, Sire, he is but a youth and as for wine he is new to it!' Hence he was p— as a 'new to it'.
Lesley Robertson, London SW4.

☐ NEWTS, like many other small creatures which were easily found in the countryside around places where beer was being brewed or cider pressed, were often added to the barrels of drink to improve flavour and strength. An article in *Tenth-Century Studies* by David Parsons remarks that the medieval practice was to put mice or weasels in beer to flavour it, but it was considered sinful to do this deliberately and cruelly drown the beasts, so the English got the priest to bless the beer first. This absolved them, since the animals were going into a holy liquid. Cider-makers in Somerset have been known to add lumps of beef to the fermenting juice, and stories circulate about rats floating in barrels of scrumpy. The newt as an

123

amphibian would survive in liquid longer than mouse, weasel and rat, and presumably would pass so much alcohol through its gills that it would soon reach that happy state wherein its grosser bodily functions would be a matter of complete indifference to it.

Angela Costen, Axbridge, Somerset.

☐ AMAZED that three people could supply different but equally mistaken answers, we feel it our duty to provide the correct answer. Abraham Newton (1631–1698) of Grantham, the presumed author of the first known treatise on the medicinal properties of the beer of Burton-upon-Trent (now unfortunately lost), was such a well-known tippler that, in his lifetime, even Londoners would use the expression 'Pissed as Abe Newton'. He was so famous that when his fellow townsman, Isaac Newton, achieved prominence, people would say of him, 'No, not that Newton.' The confusion reached its height in the early 1700s, so it was probably around this time that 'pissed as a Newton' sprang into being, only to be gradually contracted into the phrase we all know so well.

M. and B. Gidley, Exeter.

QUESTION: Why are dusters yellow?

☐ AS AN office and industrial cleaner for many years, I offer these suggestions: one of the duster's great attributes is its use for polishing. In the past, before the advent of pressurised canisters and the dreaded CFCs, this was done with beeswax. The manufacturers of such may have decided to make and sell its necessary accompaniment, dusters. Wishing to keep an identification with their main product they would naturally have dyed them yellow. Early dusters were not the bright ones of today, but a more ochre colour – indeed, some were pastel green. Alternatively: an enterprising marketing director of yesteryear may have attempted to corner the

market by using most people's association of the colour yellow with springtime, through an increase in sunshine and daylight hours. He would have realised that sales of dusters would be increased enormously by using the appropriate colour, especially during the annual spring-cleaning season. There are many examples of how the colour has become connected with spring, such as daffodils and the expression 'to be as busy as a (yellow) bee'. Spring cleaning with (yellow) wax and duster is an almost symbolic gesture of spreading sunlight around the home.
P. Millard, Bristol, Avon.

☐ IF, AS P. Millard suggests, dusters were originally coloured yellow in order to work upon the public's association of the colour with the season of spring, then the ploy will probably have been unsuccessful. Despite the increase in sunshine hours and various other yellow connotations, green and not yellow has been shown to be more commonly linked with this particular season. This was proved by the psychologist, P. H. K. Seymour, in 1976. In order to test a phenomenon of perceptual confusion known as the Stroop effect, Seymour's version of the phenomenon involved the linking of seasons and colours. In order to lay the groundwork for such an experiment, extensive testing found that the majority of people link yellow with summer, brown with autumn, white with winter, and green with spring. So if, in a few months' time, you find yourself automatically reaching for some green dusters, beware the mind-games played by *Guardian*-reading marketing directors.
Michael A. Martin, London SW20.

☐ I HAVE despaired of reading a sensible explanation for why dusters are yellow. Here is my theory instead. In the first half of the 19th century a large quantity of bright yellow cotton cloth was imported from Nanking in China, and subsequently imitated and produced in Britain, from which

highly fashionable trousers (Nankeens) were made. After the garments wore out, the remaining cloth was recycled as polishing rag in the hands of the thrifty. Yellow buckskin breeches had been fashionable earlier, and they were made of leather, cotton or wool. White linen and cotton rag was usually recycled for high quality paper, and there was never enough. I do not know if two senses of 'buff', that is (1) yellow ox-leather and (2) to polish with a piece of the same, have anything to do with the matter, but see *OED*. The traditional association between a yellow material and polishing may have reinforced the use of Nankeen cloth for dusting and cleaning after the fashion for the trousers ceased.
Charles Newton, London N22.

QUESTION: Who was the first man to do what a man's gotta do, when did he do it and what was it when he'd done it?

☐ THE words are often, wrongly, attributed to John Wayne. They were, in fact, uttered by Shane (Alan Ladd) in the film of the same name. What Shane has to do, in the conscious sense, is kill Wilson (Jack Palance) *et al.*, and pave the way for a peaceful existence for his friends, the homesteaders. However, there is an undercurrent, touched on in the movie but camouflaged by the superb action scenes and atmospheric location. It is more fully developed in the novel, *Shane*, by Jack Schaeffer, which shows that Shane is obviously in love with his friend's wife (Jean Arthur). There is also a hint that she may be falling in love with Shane while retaining her love for her husband, Joe (Van Heflin). Therefore Shane must do two things for his friends: he must rid the range of villains, at the cost of his life perhaps; and he must take himself out of their lives for ever. This is what a man has to do, and do it he does.
R. A. Southern, Wigan, Lancs.

☐ I DON'T think your correspondent is quite right in attributing the phrase to Alan Ladd in *Shane*. He uses *similar* expressions like 'A man has to be what he is' and 'I couldn't do what I gotta do', but never the exact words. The expression does occur in John Steinbeck's *Grapes of Wrath* in Chapter 18 (p. 206 of the Penguin edition) when Casy says, 'I know this – a man got to do what he got to do.' This was published in 1939, which predates *Shane* anyway. Yours pedantically, *Stephen Collins, Ripon, Yorks.*

QUESTION: What was the origin of the old debate about how many angels can dance on the head of a pin?

☐ THIS poetical and interesting question was raised by Thomas Aquinas (1225–1274). He is known as the Father of Moral Philosophy and also as the Angelic Doctor because of his preoccupation with the qualities, nature and behaviour of these celestial beings. He was canonised in 1323. *Muriel Cottrell, Wirral, Merseyside.*

☐ IT IS often used disparagingly about theological speculation. In a long past BBC Brains Trust session, the late Prof. C. E. M. Joad used the expression in that way. The following week he was firmly denounced for loose thinking by a listener who claimed, with apparent authority, that there was no evidence that this subject was ever debated. On the other hand, he said, monks in medieval times would, purely as a recreation, hold rigidly structured debates on all kinds of unlikely subjects. So the 'angels' debate could have originated from such a source. Joad had, it seemed, no answer to that. Nor have I – it just stays in the memory from the old Brains Trust days. *Stephen Fearnley, Halifax, W. Yorks.*

☐ I WAS interested to read the comments on this dispute. However, I think the idea behind it was whether angels had dimensions and occupied space. If they did not, then clearly an infinity of angels could dance on the sharpest, most needle-fine point. Milton gets round the difficulty most beautifully in Book One of *Paradise Lost* when he makes the Fallen Angels appear first 'In bigness to surpass Earth's Giant Sons' and then to 'throng numberless' in Pandemonium like tiny elves – 'incorporeal Spirits'.
Laura Garratt, Uxbridge, Middx.

QUESTION: What are the origins of the CND logo?

☐ THE symbol was originally designed by Gerald Holtom for the first Aldermaston march in 1958, organised by the Direct Action Committee Against Nuclear War. It incorporates the semaphore for N and D.
Radhika Holmstrom, Press Officer, CND, London N1.

☐ IT IS the old Nazi death sign, representing the World Ash Tree (The Tree Yssadrisil) from Nordic mythology, with its three great roots. One ended in Hel, the realm of the dead. One ended in Riesenheim, the realm of the giants. One ended in Asgard, the realm of the gods. It is illustrated in David Littlejohn's *Foreign Legions of the Third Reich*, Vol. II, page 201. In later years, CND changed the device on their badge to the 1940 divisional insignia of Hitler's 3rd Panzer division. The man responsible for CND wearing the old Nazi insignia was the late Gerald Holtom (he was also responsible for that extremely durable lie about semaphore). What his motives were we shall probably never know. It is not impossible that it was a rather sinister joke.
Shamus O. D. Wade, London W3.

QUESTION: Who first lay back and thought of England?

☐ ALICE, Lady Hillingdon, in her journal, 1912: 'I am happy now that Charles calls on my bedchamber less frequently than of old. As it is, I now endure but two calls a week and when I hear his steps outside my door I lie down on my bed, close my eyes, open my legs and think of England.'
N. G. Macbeth, Kenilworth.

QUESTION: What is the origin of the phrase 'as sick as a parrot'?

☐ TO AVOID United States quarantine and livestock importing restrictions, people smuggling parrots from South America into the US dope the birds on tequila as they near the Mexican border. Careful timing of the binge will ensure that the birds are sleeping it off through the border crossing formalities and will not greet the officials with a mouthful of verbals as is the breed's wont. Having thus avoided detection, the downside for the exotic loudmouths is coming to with the mother and father of a hangover. This queasiness manifests itself in the origin of the expression.
F. L. O'Toole, London SW19.

☐ THE phrase originates from 1926 when the previously obscure disease of bird psittacosis became a pandemic of clinical importance, involving humans in 12 countries with more than 800 cases. The association of respiratory infections in man and contact with parrots was soon recognised.
Dr F. W. A. Johnson, Liverpool.

☐ IT IS a corruption of 'sick as a pierrot' and refers to the typically pale and miserable face of that French pantomime character.
Peter Barnes, Milton Keynes.

☐ ANOTHER theory (but a quite erroneous one) is that the Amazon parrot – a large green bird with yellow cheeks – was the most-sickly-looking creature imaginable.
(Mrs) Jane M. Glossop, Pwllheli, Gwynedd.

☐ I FIRST heard this simile shortly after the Monty Python 'Norwegian Blue' sketch. Whether this is relevant, or whether it is just another example of people finding *non-sequitur* expressions of this type amusing, I know not. My mother always used to be as sick as a cowboy's 'oss. The interesting thing is that being sick as a parrot is not the same as being sick as a dog.
Alex Wilson, Billingham, Cleveland.

QUESTION: Who was Riley and why does living his life sound so desirable, in spite of dissolute overtones?

☐ THE saying comes from a comic song, 'Is That Mr Reilly?' (sic), which was popular in the US in the 1880s. There was also a music-hall song in England at about the same time: 'Are You The O'Reilly?' One was probably a variant of the other. The latter includes the lines, 'Are you the O'Reilly they speak of so highly? Cor blimey, O'Reilly, you are looking well.'
Stephen Pratt, Twyford, Berks.

QUESTION: Who was the first April Fool?

☐ THE tradition of the trickster in northern Europe goes right back to our pre-Christian religion. In the Norse mythology, the prankster-god Loki can be disruptive towards the other gods but able to carry out tasks no other can. He represents the need to question and challenge authority so that patterns of thought and behaviour do not become stale

or accepted uncritically. Loki is traditionally thought of as patron god of April.
Andy Lawton, Chesterfield, Derbys.

☐ WHEN Vasco da Gama arrived in Calicut in March 1498 (not in May as is commonly thought), he could not have known that he was creating the first documented April Fool. He was invited to the Feast of Huli, on the last day of March. The chief amusement was the be-fooling of people by sending them on fruitless and foolish errands. As any fool knows, Vasco da Gama was sent by the Hindu Rajah of Malabar inland looking for cloves and pepper in any area where they did not grow, but the event is not always attributed to the date of his return – the morning of 1 April.
A. J. G. Glossop, Pwllheli, Gwynedd.

QUESTION: Who was Kilroy when he was here, and where is he now?

☐ THE original Kilroy was an inspector at one of the inland shipyards in America where they built 'Liberty Ships'. Inspection is a responsible job, with lives depending on it. Each weld of the hull has to be inspected as it is completed, because quite often the next step will build some structure internal to the ship that will mask the weld and leave it inaccessible to later inspection. It was Kilroy's peculiar custom to record his approval of each weld by writing on the weld itself. Along decks and gangways subsequent traffic soon removed his marks, but where internal structures hid them they remained. The result was that among every crew who eventually sailed one of his ships, his became a name to conjure with, an invisible presence among them. Nobody ever met Kilroy face to face, yet he must surely be there, hiding himself away, because whenever you looked into an unused locker or enclosed space, no matter how small or inaccessible

(provided only that it backed on to the hull), he had been and gone just before you, leaving his message freshly chalked on the wall, 'Kilroy was here'.
Daniel Lowy, Sutton, Surrey.

☐ 'KILROY was here' is graffiti from the Second World War. James Kilroy was the senior shipyard inspector at the US forces shipping depot at Quincy, Massachusetts, being required to sign for all equipment consigned to ETO (European Theatre Operations). GIs, finding his name on nearly everything they used, started scrawling the phrase wherever they were based. It then spread around the world with the movement of US forces.
Bernard Goodman, London SE1.

☐ ACCORDING to an article by an American journalist, Susan Ulbing, he was an infantry soldier who got tired of hearing the Air Force brag that it was always first on the spot. Kilroy specialised in being the first and only one to show up in outrageous places, like the bathroom reserved for Truman, Stalin and Attlee at the Potsdam Conference.
John Idorn, London W8.

QUESTION: The leader of the British military mission to Russia in 1939 was Admiral Sir Reginald Plunkett-Ernle-Erle-Drax. Is this the longest hyphenated surname in the UK, and how does a man aspire to have such a surname?

☐ THE name of the explorer, Sir Ranulph Twisleton-Wykeham-Fiennes, contains more letters (33) than that queried (32), but with only three barrels to Sir Reginald's four. As to how the name was acquired, many complex names (not necessarily hyphenated) are the result of marriages,

alliances and so forth. The Fiennes family was given the name
Wykeham in the Civil War, as a reward for preventing the
desecration by the Roundheads of William of Wykeham's
tomb in Winchester Cathedral.
Arabella McIntyre Brown, Liverpool 17.

☐ OUR formal family name just beats Plunkett-Ernle-Erle-
Drax (21 letters) viz: Hovell-Thurlow-Cumming-Bruce (25
letters). Needless to say, we all abbreviate it. When I was up
at Trinity College, Cambridge, it was a curiosity much
appreciated by tourists passing the hall doors at the foot of
the staircase to my rooms to see the whole rigmarole, prefaced
'Hon. A. P.' painted upon the lintel, and followed by 'The
Earl Kitchener' and 'The Earl Jellicoe'. There's class! This
dotty accumulation derived from the 18th/19th century
usage of a husband's hyphenating his wife's name if she was
heiress to landed property. In our case H-T also then elected
to marry C-B.
Alec Cumming Bruce, Durham.

☐ IN THE event that you do not receive a suitable explanation
from a member of the Drax family, perhaps the chauffeur's
daughter can outline the cause of all the hyphens. The
admiral's ancestors were far better at breeding daughters
than sons, so that when Miss Plunkett (a relative of Lord
Dunsany – the eminent author), married Mr Ernle their
daughter was Miss Plunkett-Ernle. She married Mr Erle; their
daughter, Miss Plunkett-Ernle-Erle, married Mr Drax and
Reginald got all the surnames. After four of five daughters
Reginald begot a son, who is known as plain Mr Drax. He
has dismally failed to maintain the family tradition and has
four or five sons. His eldest son is married to the Princess
Royal's former Lady-in-Waiting, Zara (yes, that's where the
name came from) Something-Something. If she threw in her
maiden name, her children would be Something-Something-
Plunkett-Ernle-Erle-Drax. Of more value than the admiral's

abortive mission to Stalin was his pioneering interest in solar heating (for his swimming pool).
(Ms) V. E. Troy, Chatham, Kent.

☐ MY OWN name comfortably exceeds that of the gallant admiral.
(Brigadier) Dermot Hugh Blundell-Hollinshead-Blundell, BFPO 26.

☐ THE longest multi-barrelled surname on record in England is: Major Leone Sextus Denys Oswolf Fraudatifilius Tolle-mache-Tollemache-de-Orellana-Plantagenet-Tollemache-Tollemache (1884–1917). If you insist on non-repetitious ones, try this for size: Lady Caroline Jemima Temple-Nugent-Chandos-Brydges-Grenville (1858–1946).
Steve Arloff, Watford, Herts.

QUESTION: Did the Man Who Broke the Bank at Monte Carlo really exist, and if so, what was his name?

☐ HE WAS a shady American confidence trickster called Charles Deville Wells, who turned $400 into $40,000 in three days. His example inspired many, but more gamblers committed suicide at Monte Carlo than made earnings on this scale. For more information see my *Guide to Provence* (Penguin, 1989).
Michael Jacobs, London E9.

☐ HE WAS Joseph Hobson Jagger whose story is told in David James's *Victorian Bradford: The Living Past*. Jagger was an engineer who worked at Buttershaw Mill and when he visited Monte Carlo in 1875 he analysed the gearing of the roulette wheel in the casino and proceeded to win two million francs in eight days. Subsequently, Frederick Gilbert, on hearing of

Jagger's exploits, wrote the famous song 'The Man Who Broke the Bank at Monte Carlo'.
David M. Kennedy, Ilkley, Yorks.

QUESTION: What is the origin of 'The show's not over till the fat lady sings'?

☐ THE quote is, I believe, 'The game isn't over until the fat lady sings.' It comes from American baseball. At the end of a game a diva – often of Rubenesque physique – would sing 'The Star-Spangled Banner'.
David Aiken, Southall, Middx.

☐ I THINK David Aiken is wrong. The American national anthem invariably precedes a baseball game, and may be sung by almost anyone, male or female, fat or thin. According to the Library of Congress book, *Respectfully Quoted*, published last year, the phrase 'the opera ain't over till the fat lady sings' was coined in 1978 by Dan Cook, a sports writer from San Antonio, Texas, after his town's basketball team had gone one up in a championship series. He meant it as a warning, and the phrase was later popularised by the coach of the team which finally did win the series. That team was Washington, which may be why the saying entered American political jargon. It seems to reflect no more than a layman's vague idea of what happens at an opera. There is a baseball connection, however. During the worst point of their dreadful 1988 season, the Baltimore Orioles club had posters put up around the city showing an immense diva with spear and Viking helmet, and a slogan saying, 'She ain't sung yet.'
Simon Hoggart, Twickenham.

QUESTION: Where was the first banana republic, and who named it so?

☐ A BANANA republic is a politically unstable country, with an economy dependent on one or two products, such as bananas. Furthermore, this sector is dominated by one or two companies, usually foreign-owned. The classic banana republic is Honduras, which was, from the 1880s, dominated by the American-owned United Fruit and Standard Fruit companies, whose banana exports provided the republic's foreign earnings. One reluctant American expatriate in Honduras was O. Henry, the short-story writer, fleeing from the law. He spent a year there, during which time he coined the phrase 'banana republic'. However, Honduras was not the original republic to grow bananas, which had been introduced to the Canaries and West Indies many years before.
R. L. Vickers, Crewe, Cheshire.

☐ THE term is a bit of a misnomer, as two of the so-called banana republics, Nicaragua and El Salvador, produce very few, if any, bananas.
Siobhan Kenny, Glasgow.

QUESTION: What is the origin of that maddening rhythm, 'Pom tiddly-om-pom pom-pom'?

☐ ACCORDING to *The Book of World-Famous Music* by James J. Fuld, the phrase first occurs in 'Hot Scotch Rag' by H. A. Fischlet (1911). It was later used in several songs, with a variety of words added. One possible forerunner is Sullivan's setting of the words 'Shall they stoop to insult? No! No!' in *HMS Pinafore* (1878). After several bars of austere harmony, the last two words are preceded by an open octave played by a full orchestra – a strikingly bathetic cadence.
Tom McCanna, Dept. of Music, University of Sheffield.

☐ THE origin is said to be the sound of the coaches of the Chicago elevated railway (the El') running on the overhead track. Even more maddeningly they say 'shave 'n a haircut, two bits'.
(Professor) Robert Moore, Holywell, Clwyd.

QUESTION: Do the living now outnumber the dead?

☐ THE answer is no; the living population forms about 9 per cent of the total population who have ever lived, so the dead outnumber the living by about ten to one.
John Haskey, Statistician, Office of Population Studies, London.

QUESTION: Who first faded out at the end of a record, rather than having a proper ending?

☐ THE first person to fade the end of a piece of music was Gustav Holst. In the last movement of his *Planets* suite he used the gradually fading sound of a female choir to evoke the immensity of outer space. As this was written in 1915 before the introduction of electrical recording, he asked his singers to walk slowly into the distance while still singing, or for a door to be gradually closed between them and the audience. In this astonishing movement Holst anticipated the later electronic fade-out, but had in fact already used the idea as early as 1905 in his settings of songs from Tennyson's *The Princess*.
Michael Short, Bradford-on-Avon, Wiltshire.

☐ JOHANN Strauss (father) composed the 'Radetzky March' in 1848, in honour of Field Marshal Radetzky who put down Italian patriots in Milan in the same year. The fifes fade out at the end, marching away into the distance. Other members of

the Strauss family use the same device (e.g. 'Perpetuum Mobile').
G. H. Shackleton, Reading, Berks.

☐ ACCORDING to Nick Tosches in his book, *Country*, the first record to have a fade-out was 'The New Call of the Freaks', recorded by Luis Russell, the jazz musician, on 6 September 1929. This version of a tune previously recorded by Russell fades out on the added chanted refrain: 'Stick out your can, here comes the garbage man.'
David Rothon, London SW12.

☐ DUKE Ellington's 'Showboat Shuffle' (from 1935) fades away at the end but I think it was Count Basie, in the late 1930s, who started the fashion. I assume it caught on because it was a convenient way around the problem of how to end a piece. And perhaps some jazz records were faded out simply because musicians exceeded the 3 to 3½-minute time limit of the old 78s.
Sidney Evans, Chirk, Clwyd.

☐ FADE-OUTS became widespread in the United States as the result of a trade survey in the early 50s. This showed that when records were played on juke-boxes, people felt more inclined to replay a record that faded out because it left a subconscious feeling that you hadn't completely heard it. The importance of the 'juke-box factor' has never been as potent in Britain, but in the States its earning capacity has always been considerable. After the creation of the fade-out ending, the only other innovation to stimulate juke-box plays was pioneered by the Chess-Checker Record Company of Chicago, who developed a new groove-cutting technique for their 45s, which ensured that when played on juke-boxes they were one-third louder than all other records in the machine.
Dave Godin, Sheffield.

☐ THE fade has been used as an effect for many years, but it is especially suited to pop numbers, which usually consist of, or develop into, repetition of a single monotonous phrase. In consequence, the device was seized on by the groups, most of which were able to produce (one hesitates to say compose) such phrases but lacked the musical talent to bring them to an end.
David Carlé, Guildford.

QUESTION: Who said, 'There but for the grace of God go I' – and of whom was it said?

☐ JOHN Bradford, seeing a group of criminals being led out to execution, is reported to have said, 'There, but for the grace of God, goes John Bradford.' Bradford was a Protestant reformer who was born, like the *Guardian*, in Manchester. In the 1550s he was prebendary of St Paul's Cathedral and on the accession of Queen Mary he was arrested and accused of preaching seditious sermons. He was eventually burnt at the stake in June 1555.
Geoffrey T. Brown, Widnes, Cheshire.

☐ THIS quotation is ascribed to the Italian saint, Philip Neri (1515–1595). He was the founder of the Congregation of the Oratory. He had a special gift to achieve great spiritual conversions and nourish people's minds and hearts in apparently humorous ways which, while producing laughter, also purified the soul. He was well aware of his own weaknesses and that 'were it not for the grace of God' he, too, could be seeking God's pardon in the Sacrament of Reconciliation: in fact his behaviour could well become very similar to that of his penitents!
Rev. Brother L. Ryan, St Joseph's College, Stoke-on-Trent.

QUESTION: What is the origin of the phrase 'Happy as a sandboy'?

☐ A THIN layer of dry sand was spread each day on the floors of inns, taverns, ale houses etc. centuries ago to absorb the filth brought in on the footwear of the patrons. This sand carpet was spread by 'sand boys' and was swept up early the following morning before re-sanding. This fouled sand was then taken outside for riddling to separate out anything dropped by the previous day's patrons. You can imagine how delighted the sand boys would be to find the odd golden guinea and anything else of value from the sweepings. Hence the expression.
D. M. Burton, Grimsby, S. Humberside.

☐ IN THE 1840s sand boys could buy two-and-a-half tons of sand for 3s 6d and sell that quantity to all the different establishments and make between £6 and £7 per morning. When sawdust replaced sand in public houses the boys were less than happy.
A. J. Armstrong, Bexhill-on-Sea, E. Sussex.

QUESTION: Who invented traffic lights and where were the first ones situated?

☐ THE first traffic signal was invented by J. P. Knight, a railway signalling engineer. It was installed outside the Houses of Parliament in 1868 and looked like any railway signal of the time, with waving semaphore arms and red-green lamps, operated by gas, for night use. Unfortunately it exploded, killing a policeman. The accident discouraged further development until the era of the internal combustion engine. Modern traffic lights are an American invention. Red-green systems were installed in Cleveland in 1914. Three-colour signals, operated manually from a tower in the middle of the

street, were installed in New York in 1918. The first lights of this type to appear in Britain were in London, on the junction between St James's Street and Piccadilly, in 1925. They were operated manually by policemen using switches. Automatic signals, working on a time interval, were installed in Wolverhampton in 1926. The first vehicle-actuated signals in Britain occurred on the junction between Gracechurch Street and Cornhill in the City, in 1932. By some strange quirk, these were also destroyed by a gas explosion. Standardised red-amber-green signals are now universally adopted. The book *Eureka* (ed. Edward de Bono, Thames & Hudson, 1979) says: 'Boring standardisation has replaced such eccentric specimens as the elegant gilded columns of Fifth Avenue, each surmounted by a statuette, and the traffic lights of Los Angeles which, not content with changing mutely, would ring bells and wave semaphore arms to awake the slumbering motorists of the 1930s.'
Andrew McLachlan, Porthcawl, Mid-Glamorgan.

QUESTION: Why are there 60 seconds in a minute, 60 minutes in an hour and 24 hours in a day? Who decided on these time divisions?

□ THE division of the hour into 60 minutes and of the minute into 60 seconds comes from the Babylonians who used a sexagesimal (counting in 60s) system for mathematics and astronomy. They derived their number system from the Sumerians who were using it as early as 3500 BC. The use of 12 subdivisions for day and night, with 60 for hours and minutes, turns out to be much more useful than (say) 10 and 100 if you want to avoid having to use complicated notations for parts of a day. Twelve is divisible by two, three, four, six and 12 itself – whereas 10 has only three divisers – whole numbers that divide it a whole number of times. Sixty has 12 divisers and because $60 = 5 \times 12$ it combines the advantages

of both 10 and 12. In fact both 12 and 60 share the property that they have more divisers than any number smaller than themselves. This doesn't, of course, explain how this system spread throughout the world.
Phil Molyneux, London W2.

QUESTION: What is the meaning of life?

☐ IN DOUGLAS Adams's book, *The Hitch-hiker's Guide to the Galaxy*, we are informed that the computer, Deep Thought, ponders over a period of 7½ million years the question of the meaning of Life, the Universe and Everything. It is widely understood that this machine calculated the total answer to these three separate concepts as 42. Thus dividing 42 by three, it can be deduced that the meaning of life alone is 14. This, however, can only be assumed if the ratio of Life to both the Universe and Everything is 1: 1: 1.
Khairoun Abji (student at Luton VI Form College), Luton, Beds.

☐ WHAT we do know with certainty is that we were not once, are now, and will not be again.
Brian Mendes, Bromley, Kent.

☐ LIFE is a sexually transmitted condition with a 100 per cent mortality rate.
P. Mellor, Centre for Software Reliability, City University, London EC1.

☐ LIFE is not a linguistic item and hence has no meaning. The question makes as much sense as 'What is the meaning of lumbago?'
Graham Bryant, Nottingham.

☐ MY OLD pal Plotinus has it thus: 'If a man were to enquire of Nature the reason of her creative activity, and she were willing to give ear and answer, she would say, "Ask not, but understand in silence, even as I am silent and am not wont to speak." '
N. J. Crofton-Sleigh, Norwich.

☐ THE *Concise Oxford Dictionary* states that life is a 'state of functional activity and continued change peculiar to organised matter and especially to the portion of it constituting an animal or plant before death'. God knows (sic).
Jeff Thirburn, Nuneaton, Warwickshire.

☐ LIFE has no meaning related to an external frame of reference, only the meaning that you decide to give it. It follows that any such meaning given is as valid as any other for you, and any change is also up to you. Have fun being Cesare Borgia on Wednesdays and St Francis on Thursdays.
Brian Cattermole, Stevington, Beds.

☐ BEFORE directing the questioner to the nearest dictionary or his local priest I would strongly advise that this is a question not to be asked, unless rhetorically. History shows that individuals who asked this of themselves or others are prone to insanity, alcoholism or other addictions, even visions of religious ecstasy: none of these help in the least with an answer, only offering a temporary palliative for the passing of life while it is being experienced, or in providing hope for the hopeless. Matters such as destiny, happiness and other connected issues only complicate the question and should not be dragged on to the stage of reasoning. The greatest minds that have ever lived have not come near to answering this question; choose what eschatology you will for now. The chances are that whichever one you adhere to, we have all got it wrong (if only fundamentalists knew as much). This is a great mystery and long may it remain so. There is something a little dull about the prospect of knowing everything, and our humble brains are not wired for that prospect. Life is for living, surely.

James A. Oliver, London WC2.

□ ACCORDING to a BBC2 *Horizon* programme screened some years ago (not on 1 April) the meaning of life may have something to do with the notion that the most important living entity on this planet, the Earth itself, may regulate various life forms within its confines in order to ensure its own survival. Thus, for example, although the sun is now very much hotter than it was at the dawn of life, the proportion of oxygen in the atmosphere has remained more or less constant at 21 per cent, any greater or lesser amount being catastrophic. This suggests some kind of self-regulating mechanism which may be provided by the gases, particularly from manure, of all living things. That would also explain various epidemics and natural disasters, as Mother Earth controls the number of living creatures and thus the level and mixture of atmospheric gases. What the meaning of life is for Planet Earth is another matter.

D. Fisher, Maidenhead, Berks.

QUESTION: Does anybody know the origin of the hammer and sickle as a political symbol? I was once informed by a work colleague that it originated among Russian exiles in America, but have never been able to prove or refute this theory.

□ THIS clearly symbolises the rule of the proletariat, industrial and rural. But it may well be an adaptation of a much older Russian symbol: that of the cross above the upturned crescent, celebrating the triumph of Christianity

over Islam. This can still be seen crowning one of the domes of St Basil's Cathedral in Moscow.
D. R. Howison, Oakham, Rutland.

☐ D. R. HOWISON is wrong on two counts. The sickle represents not the 'rural proletariat' but the peasantry. 'Rural proletarians' are wage labourers with no direct interest in the land they farm, and only a tiny fraction of the rural population in pre-revolutionary Russia. This may seem a quibble, but it was a vital factor in Lenin's revolutionary strategy. Nor is the hammer-and-sickle emblem based (other than perhaps unconsciously) on the crescent surmounted by the cross. The Bolsheviks would have had no desire to elevate the Orthodox Church above Islam, and in any case the Communist emblem would require a 45-degree rotation to bear even a passing resemblance to the anti-Islamic one. The hammer and sickle was in fact a simplified development of the earlier emblem of the Russian Social-Democratic Labour Party (Bolsheviks) which appeared on the 1918 propaganda poster, 'Denikin's Band', as the hammer crossed with the plough. This emblem also appeared within the red star of the earliest cap badges of the Red Army. Unfortunately I cannot name its originator, or say whether it was ever an official state emblem. By the time of the founding of the USSR, it had been completely replaced by the simpler and more easily recognised hammer and sickle.
Denver Walker, Bristol.

☐ THE origins are obscure, but according to Stephen White, an authority on Bolshevik iconography, the famous symbol of unity between workers and peasants first made its appearance in Saratov in 1917 as the emblem of the local Soviet. It swiftly became popular and by July 1918 the first Soviet constitution adopted it as the state symbol of the RSFSR.
John Gorman, Waltham Abbey, Essex.

QUESTION: Where, when and by whom were semi-detached houses first built?

☐ I DO not know where the first semi-detached house was built, but I have it on reliable authority that the second one was built just next door to the first.
George James, Shepperton, Middx.

☐ THE origin of the semi-detached house, at least in London, is explained in *The Book of London*, which I edited for Weidenfeld. The Georgian terrace held sway until the last decade of the 18th century, when inflationary pressures pushed up building costs and left some terraces uncompleted – similar to the problems today in Docklands. Building houses in self-contained pairs meant that it was easier to stop when the money ran out. The architect and developer, Michael Searles, is credited with London's earliest semis, built in Kennington Park Road in the early 1790s. He followed these with a development in Greenwich and the Paragon in Blackheath. Then, as now, south London was at the cutting edge of innovation.
Michael Leapman, London SW8.

☐ MICHAEL Leapman is nearly there – but not quite. Architect Michael Searles (a Greenwich man) may well have been inspired by the pair of houses built in Blackheath in 1776 by Thoman Gayfere and John Groves, both of Westminster. The houses, which stand today on the west edge of the Heath and are known as Lydia and Sherwell, are by legend the first semi-detached houses certainly in London. That is, if you take the meaning of semi-detached to be two houses consciously designed to look from a distance like one. Pevsner/Cherry in their book, *London 2: South*, give the Gayfere/Groves houses the accolade. It is a credit which we at the Blackheath Society will stoutly defend. Searles' first semis followed about 30 years later.

But if it is the terrace form in question, then Searles is your man.
Neil Rhind for The Blackheath Society, London SE5.

☐ SORRY, Blackheath! Richard Gillow of Lancaster (1734–1811) was designing 'semis' or pairs of houses in that town as early as 1758/9, in Moor Lane. The earliest identifiable surviving pair is that built in 1760 at Fleet Bridge (now facing the bus station and partly demolished) for Captain Henry Fell. These are very similar to a pair in St Leonardsgate which may be the buildings designed by Gillow in 1765/6 for Edward Salisbury. Captain Fell occupied one of his houses himself but the others were built to be let. Gillow obtained estimates of £110 for building William Braithwaite's houses in Moor Lane in 1759 and reckoned they would let for £4 per annum each. *Pace* Pevsner, no legend here: the evidence is in the Gillow archives in Westminster Public Library. Richard Gillow was the son of the founder of the cabinet-making dynasty, and seems to have studied architecture in London. From 1757 to the 1770s he provided designs for numerous public and private buildings in the Lancaster area. The architectural work of Richard Gillow was the subject of my dissertation at Cambridge in 1982. I used the Gillow archives to establish beyond doubt that Richard Gillow designed a considerable number of buildings in this period.
P. A. Harrison, London SW16.

☐ SORRY, Blackheath! Sorry, Richard Gillow of Lancaster. What must surely be counted as the first pair of semi-detached houses, nos 808–810 Tottenham High Road, London N17, date from 1715–1725 – thus predating Gillow's work by something like 50 years. This pair of houses makes a noble and remarkably balanced visual ensemble still, despite later shopfronts. For an illustration see Dan Cruickshank and Peter Wyld's fascinating *London: the Art of Georgian Building.*
Philip Maher, Marston, Oxford.

☐ IT WAS always my belief that the semi-detached dwelling originated in the ancient Inca civilisation of South America. This novel idea greatly impressed the Spanish Conquistadores, who brought the concept to Europe in the 16th century, and gave it the name 'Casa Doble'.
Vaughan R. Hully, Warley, W. Midlands.

☐ SUMMERSON'S *Georgian London* states that the Eyre Estate in St John's Wood 'was the first part of London, and indeed of any other town, to abandon the terrace house for the semi-detached villa – a revolution of striking significance and far-reaching effect.' One reason why the semi-detached house was so frequently built between the wars was that motor buses could still operate profitably in new, less densely developed suburbs where passenger loadings would have been too low to justify building new tramways and railways. Another reason was that Town and Country Planning zoning introduced in new suburbs from 1909 onwards provided for different residential areas to be developed at varying densities, usually between four and 12 houses per acre. Plots in the middle zones were too small for detached houses but too large for terraces and therefore most suitable for semi-detached houses. The archetypal outer London semi may appear more prevalent than it really is because some developers erected semi-detached houses on the principal main road frontages but built terraces in the hinterland.
John Tarling, London SW15.

☐ THE semi-detached houses identified by your correspondents are all far too modern. Here in Cornwall we have a pair of semis dating from the Roman occupation of Britain, in the second and third centuries AD. The stone-walled village of Chysauster near Penzance had the remains of a house which clearly takes the form of two semi-detached dwellings.
D. Stewart, Helston, Cornwall.

☐ I THINK Warwick can go one better than Blackheath, Lancaster and Tottenham in that it can boast a pair of semi-detached houses which date from the late 1690s. The impressive building, which stands near the site of the old Northgate into the town, looks like one house but is in fact two, divided by a central carriageway.

Amanda Clarke, Warwick.

☐ IF A semi-detached house is one which was designed as a symmetrically arranged pair there are several surviving examples in Coventry, dating back at least to the 14th century. Nos 169–170 Spon Street, Coventry, which was repaired under the supervision of the architect F. W. B. Charles in 1969–70 for the City of Coventry under the Spon Street Townscape scheme, is a good example of 14th-century date. Further along Spon Street is a 16th-century three-storey pair of town houses at 8–10 Much Park Street which was dismantled and reconstructed by Mr Charles on its present site in 1971–74. Both these examples had houses built up against them, as the street frontage filled up, and we feel sure that there must be many earlier examples which have become absorbed within later terraced development along urban streets. On the principle of originally detached, subsequently attached, we would be interested in hearing how common this type of 'semi' was in medieval towns.

George Demidowicz, Conservation Officer, City of Coventry.

QUESTION: Who was 'nosey' Parker?

☐ THE first supplement to the *Oxford English Dictionary* credits Compton Mackenzie with the earliest use of the expression in his 1912 novel, *Carnival*: 'I saw you go off with a fellah.' 'What of it, Mr Nosey Parker?' This was only two years after the earliest cited example of 'nosey' in the sense

of 'inquisitive, curious', as used by H. G. Wells in *The History of Mr Polly*. So the expression seems to have derived from early 20th-century slang. However, I well remember as a lad an illustrated and informative item in a magazine which said that the original Nosey Parker was Matthew Parker, Elizabeth I's first Archbishop of Canterbury. I can find no confirmation of this in the hagiographic entry on him in the *Dictionary of National Biography* or any other reference work I have been able to consult. The *OED* would have us believe that 'nosey' could not have been used in any sense as early as the 16th century: 1. 'One who has a large nose' is apparently not known before 1788; 2. 'Evil smelling', 1836; 3. 'Fragrant', 1892; 4. 'Sensitive to bad smells', 1894.
(Dr) Richard Dutton, Dept. of English, Lancaster University.

☐ MATTHEW Parker, who was Archbishop of Canterbury (1559–75), had rather a reputation for prying into the affairs of others. He therefore acquired the nickname 'Nosey Parker'.
William H. Watts, Leighton Buzzard, Beds.

QUESTION: When did the first 'Disgusted of Tunbridge Wells' letter appear in a newspaper? Why was he/she disgusted?

☐ I SEEM to recall that this was used in letters of complaint by Jimmy Edwards in the old 'Take It From Here' radio programme.
Rita Kiernan, Nailsea, Bristol.

☐ THE expression might have something to do with Dr William Webber, who caused the 'Webber Riots' in the town in 1864. He complained to the Home Office about a drain –

see my book, *Royal Tunbridge Wells: A Pictorial History* (Phillimore 1990).
Roger Farthing, Tunbridge Wells, Kent.

☐ THE editor of the *Female Tatler*, which first appeared in July 1709, asked her readers to send her 'the ridiculous things that happen at Epsom, Tunbridge and the Bath'. In August she referred to a letter from a lady in Tunbridge – 'a place resorted to by Persons with a Design to be as ill-tempered and censorious as they possibly can'. Among such persons, it appears, were Lady Carper and Mrs Undermine.
Helen Mead, Oxford.

QUESTION: Who tested the first parachute and did he live to tell the tale?

☐ DISREGARDING Chinese acrobats who, in order to entertain the emperor in the 16th century, were supposed to have jumped from various heights with umbrellas attached to themselves, and Fausto Veranzio of Venice who is supposed to have tested a crude form of parachute in 1616, it is generally accepted that Sebastian le Normand of Montpellier in France was the first person to test a parachute. This he did on Boxing Day in 1783, jumping from the tower of Montpellier Observatory, attached to a rigid parachute made of canvas and wicker-work. He landed safely. Balloonists developed and refined this form of rigid parachute and made numerous descents, with varying degrees of success, as part of the general entertainment associated with ballooning. The originator of the folded parachute, capable of being stored in a container and opening on descent, was Major Thomas Baldwin of the US who, in 1850, began successful demonstrations of his equipment, again by dropping from a balloon. However, the parachutes suffered from the limitation that they were attached to the balloon and were only opened by

means of the parachutist dropping away, pulling the parachute from its container and, when fully extended, breaking the cord attaching the parachute to the balloon. The reputed inventor of the self-contained manually opened parachute capable of being worn about a person's body was Leo Stevens of the US who, in 1908, is said to have demonstrated such a parachute, though it was not until the First World War that such parachutes became generally available.
Steve Day, Salisbury, Wilts.

QUESTION: What is the derivation of the term 'round robin'?

☐ AN EARLY use of the term was aboard 18th-century ships. Conditions were often very bad, and crews were known to mutiny. Sometimes this would take the form of a petition to the captain asking for better treatment. The usual reaction of the captain was to look for the name at the top of the left-hand column, and hang him from the yardarm. To get round this, the crew would instead sign a 'round robin' in the shape of a circle. This, however, did not help much, because the captain would then take reprisals against the man whose name was in the 12 o'clock position (known as the 'ringleader'). Apart from the obvious alliteration, I do not know why it should be called a 'robin'.
Keith Trobridge, Shipley, W. Yorks.

☐ AN EARLIER use of the term was as a blasphemous name for the sacrament, *c.* 1555: 'There were at Paules fixed railing bils against the Sacrament, terming it Jacke of ye boxe, the sacrament of the halter, round Robin, with lyke unseemely termes.' (Ridley, quoted in *Oxford English Dictionary.*)
Frank Cummins, Warley, W. Midlands.

QUESTION: Why 'Piggy Bank'? Why not lamb, cow or donkey bank?

☐ THIS originates from about the 16th century. The pig is the only farm animal that is of value only when dead. Thus the 'bank', traditionally made out of china, was so designed that it had to be broken in order to be opened – symbolically 'killing the pig'. Other farm animals do not have to be killed before they are of use. For instance, the cow can be milked, the bull put to stud, eggs obtained from hens and so on.
R. Thomas, Bridgend, Mid-Glamorgan.

☐ IT APPEARS that livestock farming is not R. Thomas's forte. Sows and boars produce progeny, like cows and bulls, ewes and rams. Like fattening pigs, fattening cattle and fattening lambs are also 'of value only when dead', to use Mr Thomas's unfortunate phrase, which is also, however, a far from accurate statement. Perhaps the answer is simpler: because it was only this little piggy that went to market?
John Nix, Emeritus Professor of Farm Business Management, Wye College, Ashford, Kent.

☐ AT ONE time, people used to keep their money in pots made of a type of earthenware called pigge. These so-called 'pigge banks' were not at first made in the shape of pigs, but presumably some manufacturer thought it was funny to do so.
Peter Morris, Norwich.

☐ THE pig is an ancient symbol of worldly wealth throughout China and Southeast Asia. Pottery models of pigs were made as funerary offerings and were often stuffed with paper 'money' specially made for funerary purposes. The earliest example of a piggy-bank I have seen is a 12th–13th century Majapahit terracotta of a very chubby pig from Java. It is hollow, with a thin slot in the top of its back. Similar piggy-

banks were produced in Java and Sumatra between the 12th and 17th centuries. Since the earliest European example I have seen is an early Delft blue and white piggy bank dating from around 1610, I have always assumed that the Dutch imported the design from Indonesia.
Nigel Palmer, London SW15.

QUESTION: What is the origin of the crescent moon symbol seen throughout Islamic cultures?

☐ ISLAM emerged in Arabia where travel along the desert trade routes was largely by night, and navigation depended upon the position of the moon and stars. The moon thus represents the guidance of God on the path through life. The new moon also represents the Muslim calendar, which has 12 months each of 29 or 30 days. So in Islam the lunar month and the calendar month coincide, and the new moon is eagerly awaited, especially at the end of the month of Ramadan when its sighting means that the celebrations of 'Id al-Fitr can begin.
Linda and Phil Holmes, Cottingham, N. Humberside.

☐ THE use of the so-called crescent moon in many Islamic symbols cannot be related to the importance attached to the new moon in Islam. The moon depicted on e.g. many Islamic flags is the old moon, the reverse shape of the new moon, which is like a letter C backwards. Again 'crescent', implying 'increasing', is properly applicable only to the young moon: the old moon is diminishing in phase. Presumably the moon is depicted as a crescent in Islamic, and many other, contexts as that shape is unambiguously lunar.
A. A. Davis, London SW7.

☐ ALTHOUGH the crescent is indeed a very widespread motif in Islamic iconography, it is not Islamic in origin nor exclusive

to that religion. The emblem has been used in Christian art for many centuries in depictions of the Virgin Mary, for example. It is in fact one of the oldest icons in human history, having been known in graphic depictions since at least as early as the Babylonian period in Mesopotamia. The stele of Ur Namu, for example, dating from 2100 BC, includes the crescent moon to symbolise the god Sin, along with a star representing Shamash, the sun god. Later the moon became a female deity, typified by the goddess Artemis and her many counterparts, including Diana, who was celebrated as the moon-goddess in Roman times and depicted with a crescent on her brow. The device seems to have entered Islam via the Seljuk Turks who dominated Anatolia in the 12th century, and was widely used by their successors, the Ottoman Turks, who eventually became the principal Islamic nation and whose Sultan held the title of Caliph until 1922. The story that the Ottomans adopted the crescent to symbolise their conquest of Constantinople must be dismissed as mere legend, since the device considerably predates 1453. In the late 19th century the Pan-Islamic movement sponsored by the Sultan Abdul Hamid II used the crescent and star on a green flag as part of its propaganda, and from this were derived the flags of Egypt and Pakistan and many other Islamic states.
William G. Crampton, Director of the Flag Institute, Chester.

☐ A DETAILED answer will be found in the entry 'Hilal', *Encyclopaedia of Islam* (second edition, Brill, Leiden, 1960). Professor Richard Ettinghausen, writer of the entry, notes that the crescent moon (hilal) motif is featured with a five- or six-pointed star (the latter known as Solomon's shield in the Islamic world) on early Islamic coins circa AD 695, but it carried no distinct Islamic connotation. Some 500 years later, it appears in association with various astrological/astronomical symbols on 12th-century Islamic metal-work, but when depicted in manuscript painting, held by a seated man, it is thought to represent the authority of a high court official: 'the sun [is] to the king and the moon [is] to the vizier . . .' Its use as a roof finial on Islamic buildings also dates from this medieval period, but the motif still had no specific religious meaning as it decorated all types of architecture, secular as well as religious. In fact Ettinghausen argues that it was the European assumption that this was a religious and national emblem which led to several Muslim governments adopting it officially during the 19th century.

(Dr) Patricia Baker, Farnham, Surrey.

QUESTION: Are scientists any closer to answering the question: which came first, the chicken or the egg?

☐ ASSUMING that the chicken evolved from two other birds which were not quite chickens, then these two latter birds must have produced, at some time in the past, an egg out of which came the first chicken.

Geoffrey Samuel, Lancaster.

☐ WE MUST remember that the chicken is an *actual* chicken whereas the egg is only a *potential* chicken. Philosophically speaking, actuality always precedes potentiality, so the chicken came first. Probably.

Kishor Alam, London N14.

☐ KISHOR Alam argues on the basis of actuality preceding potentiality that the chicken must come before the egg. But from the egg's point of view, a chicken is only a potential egg (just as human beings are simply the way genes manage to perpetuate themselves).

David Lewis, St Albans, Herts.

☐ THE chicken is, of course, *Archaeopteryx*, the oldest fossil bird. It comes from the Solnhofen Lithographic Limestone,

from the late Jurassic rocks of Bavaria (that is about 150 million years ago). Its skeleton is so like that of contemporary dinosaurs that it is generally agreed that its ancestors were in fact small, lightly built dinosaurs. The dinosaurs were reptiles, and in some cases are known to have laid eggs, therefore it is likely that the egg came first. However, most fossil reptile eggs date from the later Cretaceous period (144 to 65 million years ago) and are those of large dinosaurs – large and relatively strong eggs which have a better chance of preservation than smaller ones. The oldest find reported (from the Early Permian – about 270 million years ago – of Texas) is so poorly preserved that palaeontologists are uncertain about its true identity. It may be the remains of an inorganic nodule – a chemical growth within the sediment. The earliest reptile fossils come from even older rocks: the Early Carboniferous (350 million years ago) of Scotland. So it is probable that the earliest eggs date from this time – 200 million years before *Archaeopteryx*. The egg is no chicken!
(Dr) Denis Bates, Institute of Earth Studies, University College of Wales, Aberystwyth.

☐ READERS may be interested in the rather tongue-in-cheek article by Walter N. Thurman and Mark E. Fisher: 'Chicken, Eggs, and Causality, or Which Came First?' (*American Journal of Agricultural Economics*, May 1988). The authors conducted so-called 'Granger causality tests' using annual data from the US Department of Agriculture on egg production and chicken population covering the period 1930–83. Such tests can be used to see if there is an asymmetry between the value of the information provided by past observations of the variables in predicting each other's current values. Using regression analysis one attempts to discover whether variations in a series Y (say chicken population) can be adequately explained by its own past values, or whether lagged values of a second variable X (say egg production) contribute significantly to the equation. A similar regression would be carried out reversing the role of the variables. If it can be shown that X is needed to help explain Y (after accounting for the influence of past values of Y) but that Y is not needed to explain movements in X, then one may conclude that X 'Granger-causes' Y (after Clive Granger who first proposed the procedure). Using this approach in what Thurman and Fisher called 'the most natural application of tests for Granger causality', they concluded that the egg came first. However, readers may feel that this result should be taken with a pinch of salt, especially when they hear that other applications of the test have given rise to such perverse findings as 'GNP "causes" sunspot activity'!

Guy Judge, Emsworth, Hants.

QUESTION: What is the origin of the mortar-board headgear worn by graduates?

☐ IN THE European universities of the 12th century it was customary to award the graduating scholar a special cap, which was known variously as a pileus or biretta. It appears originally to have been a plain round bonnet crowned with a small tuft, or apex, and was worn over a skull-cap or coif. Around the year 1500 it became fashionable to pinch the crown of the cap into four corners, allegedly to represent the sign of the cross (universities were ultimately under the authority of the Pope). This came to be known as the pileus quadratus ('square cap'), and was referred to in English as the cater-cap or corner-cap. In some instances the cap developed into a more rigid, formalised headgear. Among Catholic clerics it became the biretta, still worn today, and the fins on its crown recall the quartering on the original pileus. Meanwhile in England, by the end of the 17th century, in the academic world the same cap had been reduced to a square of pasteboard covered with black serge and attached to a rigid skull-cap. This was the forerunner of the modern

mortar-board. The original soft, flat cap is still worn by many female graduates and by female members of numerous church choirs.
J. P. Fortune, London SW6.

QUESTION: 'Bob's your uncle.' Who is Bob?

☐ ROBERT Arthur Talbot Gascoyne-Cecil, third Marquess of Salisbury and Prime Minister in 1887, when he promoted (not for the first time) his nephew A. J. Balfour to be Chief Secretary for Ireland in a move widely interpreted as an unusually literal act of nepotism. Balfour himself later became Prime Minister, and later still the Foreign Secretary who made the Balfour Declaration in 1917. Originally 'Bob's your uncle' was presumably an ironic or jocular catchphrase meaning 'It's all right for you' (i.e. you've got an Uncle Bob), though now it has lost its tone.
B. A. Phythian, Keston, Kent.

QUESTION: Why, when a footballer scores three goals in a game, is it called a 'hat-trick'?

☐ THE term originated in cricket and refers to the bowler's taking of three wickets in successive balls. George Macdonald Frazer (*Flashman's Lady*, set in 1843) claims the first use for Flashman. When he takes his third wicket (by cheating), the victim, Alfred Mynn, presents Flashman with his straw boater as he leaves the field with the words: 'That trick's worth a new hat any day, youngster.' More seriously, Eric Partridge (*Historical Slang*), giving 1882 as the probable date of origin, says it entitled its professional performer to a collection, or to a new hat from his club. Amateur players, being gentlemen, could, presumably, afford their own hats.
Ramin Minova, Moseley, Birmingham.

☐ DAVID Harris, the great Hambledon bowler of the 1780s, was presented with a gold-laced hat after a fine spell of bowling, though not actually taking three wickets with successive deliveries. Around 1800 the first top hat, a white beaver, came into vogue and was awarded by some clubs to bowlers who took three wickets with successive deliveries. This practice grew until the late 1800s when the tasselled cap, boater and pill-box cap made the top hat no longer de rigueur. The hat-trick was then coined by other sports to indicate a three-fold success.
Steve Pittard, Langport, Somerset.

☐ WHEN football was in its infancy, and hence footballers were not professional, top scorers were not rewarded for their goals. If a player scored three goals in a match, a hat, or similar container, would be passed round for donations. I presume that only the home supporters would actually chip in.
Peter Orme, Winchester, Hants.

QUESTION: Why, in general, do women live longer than men?

☐ EVIDENCE suggests that boys are the weaker sex at birth, with a higher infant mortality rate, and women seem to have a better genetic resistance to heart disease than men. The process of gender role socialisation means men are more likely to be brought up to 'shrug off' illnesses, they drink and smoke more, they are more aggressive and take more risks, are less careful in what they eat and are not socialised to show their emotions as much as women and so have less outlet for stress. Women are socialised to 'take care of themselves' more than men, and they are more likely to visit doctors, which may mean they receive better health care. Men generally live more hazardous lives than women. The more dangerous occupations, such as construction work, are likely to be done by men and they are therefore more at risk of industrial accidents and diseases. In the home, men are more likely to do the dangerous and risky jobs, such as using ladders and climbing on the roof. Men also make up the majority of car drivers and motorcyclists (63 per cent in 1990) and are therefore more at risk of death through road accidents. Men are more likely to work full-time and to work longer and more unsociable hours, such as overtime working and shift-work, which can be harmful to health. Jobs carrying high levels of responsibility are more commonly done by men, which may cause higher levels of health-damaging stress. Men retire later than women (age 65 compared with 60) and this may also be an important factor in reducing their life expectation.

Ken Browne, Leamington Spa, Warwicks.

☐ KEN Browne fails to mention the most important influence on women's longevity: the tremendous reduction of death during or after childbirth in the last 100 years. Historically, women died in childbirth, men in wars, and both in agricultural accidents. Hence philosophers and nuns lived to a great age. Leaving aside the question of whether too much work is bad for you, it is not true that men work longer hours than women: all the evidence is that women have less leisure time than men because they still do most of the work in the home, whether or not they have a job. It is also an error to state that jobs carrying high levels of responsibility are necessarily more stressful. Studies of production-line workers have shown that repetitive tasks can produce high levels of stress. My grandfather, in an interview with the local paper on his sixtieth wedding anniversary (when both he and his wife were 90) attributed his longevity to 'hard work and eating sparingly'. They were teetotal Methodists and didn't smoke, but then not everyone would want to go 90 years without a drink.

Jacqueline Castles, London W2.

QUESTION: Given the availability of all known building materials and ideal rock to build on, what would be the height of the highest building that could be built today? What would be the constraining factor?

☐ With an infinite budget the normal limits of high-rise construction are removed. Loading can safely be distributed into the world's strongest bedrock using massive foundations. Overall stability against wind loading and buckling will be assured if the building is allowed enough ground to be self-bracing. So, in pure structural terms, the controlling factor is the ability of the building frame to carry vertical loading. Assuming the building is a residential block (office loading is greater) and using solid steel columns of sensible style and spacing, to allow the building to be properly inhabited, an overall height of about 1,250 metres (450 storeys) is possible. A steel 'Eiffel' tower about 4,000 metres high is possible. I hope you realise that we are a few years too late to get funding for this type of development.
Ian Hunt, London N10.

☐ If we define buildings as man-made edifices above ground and containing spaces allowing humans to move about within the structure, then the pyramids of Egypt and Central America are buildings. Mount Everest is a natural pyramid; therefore, using granite blocks a conical or pyramidal building could be erected to a height of at least 10,000 metres. The actual constraining factors would be geological. Isostatic downwarping of the crust beneath the enormous weight of the structure would cause faults in the rock mass, while metamorphic processes at the core of the pyramid (melting of certain minerals in the granite due to pressure) would result in instability and collapse. These constraints could be overcome by giving the building a honeycomb or lattice structure and using a variety of lighter and more tensile materials than granite. Living spaces within the cone/

pyramid could be provided, so creating a city perhaps tens of thousands of metres high. There would be increasing problems in supplying the higher levels with water, fuel, waste disposal and so forth and there would be complex ecological and climatic challenges to the architects. But perhaps the ultimate constraining factor is human nature: the general unpopularity of high-rise flats and the biblical myth of the Tower of Babel suggest why such a conical mega-city could not succeed.
Michael Ghirelli, Hillesden, Bucks.

QUESTION: Who was the original buck passer and what was the buck that was passed?

☐ THE riverboats which travelled the Mississippi and Missouri rivers in the last century did more than take settlers West to join their wagon trains. They linked the major cities up and down what remains today a vital inland trade route. They also carried many less reputable travellers, including show-men and gamblers. When playing poker it is quite common for each hand to be dealt by a different player. Sometimes, as the dealer changed, so did the rules. This made cheating more difficult and the game far more interesting. As the deal moved around the group, the dealer's job was marked by placing a knife on the table in front of the man with the cards. Often this knife had a handle made from the antler of a male deer or buck: a Buck Knife. 'Passing the buck' thus came to mean passing the responsibility for control of the game to someone else. It was probably Harry Truman, a son of the town of Independence by the Missouri river, who introduced the term to the rest of the United States, with the famous sign on his Oval Office desk which read 'The Buck Stops Here'.
Jeremiah Sheehan, London SE15.

QUESTION: Who was the first socialist?

☐ IT'S THE wrong question. Socialism came first, and private property later. So the question should have been, 'Who invented private property?' Ancient Jewish tradition blamed Cain. Not only a murderer, he committed the second crime of instituting private property in land: he 'set bounds to fields'. The ancient world looked back with longing to the Golden Age of Saturn when all things were held in common: 'No fences parted fields, nor marks nor bounds Divided acres of litigious grounds, But all was common.' (Virgil, *Georgics I* (125–128).) Plato applauded simple communism but said it would fail because of the lowest part of human nature. Lactantius, in the reign of Diocletian, condemned private property, and the early Christian Fathers like St Cyprian, Clement of Alexandria, Tertullian etc. all advocated common ownership.
Karl Heath, Coventry.

☐ AROUND AD 532, during the rule of Khosro Anoushirvan, the king of the Sasanians, a man called Mazdak founded a communistic sect which made headway among the people, especially the poor. Mazdak demanded that the rich should live less luxuriously and should distribute their wealth among the poor. Khosro condemned the Mazdakites, who were butchered in 528 by planting them in the soil upside down or cutting off their heads.
Behrouz Kia, Istanbul, Turkey.

QUESTION: Who first 'lost his bottle'?

☐ SHAKESPEARE wrote about lager louts in the early 17th century in *The Tempest*, Act IV, Scene 1. After a drunken and fruitless chase across wild marshland led by the 'monster' Caliban, the bedraggled Trinculo bemoans the fact that he

and Stephano have sunk so low as 'to lose our bottles in the pool'. Stephano agrees – 'There is not only disgrace and dishonour in that, monster, but an infinite loss.'
Colin Morley, Totteridge, London N20.

☐ THE 'bottle' is, in full, the Cockney rhyming slang 'bottle and glass'. The 'loss' refers to the control of the anal sphincter in moments of great danger or stress. From this, we can deduce that Adam was the first to experience this unpleasant occurrence, when called to account in the Garden of Eden.
Joseph Cramp, Clayhall, Essex.

QUESTION: We are led by the Gospels to understand that Christ and his disciples lived and dressed simply – so what gave rise to the tradition of magnificent palaces and gorgeous vestments, and when did it start?

☐ THROUGHOUT the New Testament period and beyond, the Christian Church continued to meet in dwelling-houses or modest buildings privately owned. When, in the 4th century AD, the Emperor Constantine accepted the legal existence of the Church throughout the Empire, it was officially able to own property and to receive legacies. From this time onwards, some great palaces and basilicas were given to the Church by wealthy benefactors, whose names and portraits have survived within the buildings themselves. Certain bishops were admitted to the Imperial court, and they dressed accordingly. Many of the vestments worn today by ecclesiastical dignitaries resemble the court fashions of the Late Roman and Byzantine periods. There have been attempts within the various branches of the Church to re-establish the practice of poverty – notably that of St Francis of Assisi, when he founded the Franciscan Order in the 13th century. Even at a High Mass in St Peter's, Rome, the Pontiff discards

his extra adornments and approaches the altar in simple garments such as Jesus would have worn in his earthly life.
J. M. Frayn, Kingston-on-Thames, Surrey.

QUESTION: Why is the control area of an aircraft called the cockpit?

☐ A COCKPIT was a small dugout circle enclosed by wooden rails and used for cock-fighting, a popular 17th-century sport. Similar structures came to be called a cockpit by analogy: for example, the Cockpit Theatre, which would often feature bloody scenes on its confined stage. Later, the back part of the orlop deck of a man-o'-war became known as the cockpit. It was narrow and deep, with wooden railings, and there was another connection with blood – during battle, wounded sailors were transferred to it. This opened up new meanings for cockpit linked to travel, while retaining the idea of a confined space. In some ship designs the cockpit was also used for navigation. Travel in narrow, deep spaces was a feature of early aircraft. And the language of flying picked up many terms from seafaring – aeronautics, knots, navigation. So the 'cockpit' was borrowed to refer to the confined space in the fuselage for crew and passengers. Later it was specialised to mean the pilot's area.
Doug Gowan, Hornsey, London N8.

QUESTION: According to encyclopaedias, the rhinoceros has roamed the earth for 70 million years. If dinosaurs became extinct about 60 million years ago, why did the rhinoceros survive?

☐ IT IS probably simplistic to assume that dinosaurs (there were more than 100 families of them) died out suddenly 65 million years ago, destroyed by asteroids or meteorites. The

most likely explanation is a gradual decline brought about by climatic change, which mammals like the ancestors of the rhino were able to exploit to their advantage. Mammals evolved from mammal-like reptiles between 250 and 200 million years ago, so dinosaurs and mammals co-existed over a period of nearly 200 million years. In this time, many dinosaur families – the anchisaurids, brachiosaurids, diplocids etc. simply died out. So mammals, birds, reptiles and amphibians are dinosaurs that have adapted to changing conditions. The evolution of the rhinoceros may provide part of the answer to this evolutionary conundrum. The rhinos of Africa and the tapirs of South America are related: their common ancestor was possibly *Indricotherum* from Asia, which was 18 feet high at the shoulder and weighed 32 tons. It died out in the Miocene period. Later in the Miocene, the horned rhino evolved: sub-species included the Woolly Rhinoceros and the *Brontotherium*. These latter were ecologically replaced by the giant rhinos of the late Oligocene, about 35 million years ago.
Robert Turpin, Peverell, Plymouth.

□ BOTH the question and the given answer are in error. Rhinoceroses have certainly not 'roamed the earth for 70 million years'. Ancestral rhinoceroses have been found in deposits of the late Eocene age (about 40 million years old), whilst the dinosaurs died out 65 million years ago at the end of the Cretaceous period. Therefore a gap of about 20 million years separates the dinosaurs from the line of mammals that gave rise to the rhinos of today. Rhinos and tapirs are closely related, but *Indricotherium* was not the 'common ancestor' of the two groups. *Indricotherium* was in fact an early offshoot of the lineage that gave rise to modern rhinos. Also, the woolly rhino (*Coelodonta*) could not have been ecologically replaced by the '. . . rhinos of the Oligocene', as the woolly rhino lived during the Pleistocene, 21 million years after the end of the Oligocene! Although dinosaurs were on the decline before they finally became extinct, we cannot at present (if ever) assign this with a single cause. The world's climate was changing at the end of the Cretaceous period, and there is good evidence of an asteroid impact 65 million years ago. However, the relative importance of these factors (and other environmental and biological changes occurring at the same time) is a matter of great contention. Finally, the following statement: 'So mammals, birds, reptiles and amphibians are dinosaurs that have adapted to changing conditions,' is just not true. The dinosaurs were a distinct group of animals. It is thought that some small carnivorous dinosaurs are ancestral to birds, but living mammals and amphibians are only distantly related to the dinosaurs. In fact it is thought that dinosaurs are more closely related to birds than to living 'reptiles' (turtles, lizards and snakes, and crocodiles).

Paul M. Barrett, Department of Earth Sciences, University of Cambridge.

QUESTION: Who was the last person to be beheaded in this country? Was an official decision made to stop the practice?

☐ SIMON, Lord Lovat, was the last person beheaded in England (9 April 1747). Beheading is said to have been introduced into England by William the Conqueror in the 11th century, and the punishment was usually reserved for offenders of high rank. (The ancient Greeks and Romans regarded it as a more honourable form of execution too.) The fourth Earl Ferrers was hanged after a petition (1760) to be beheaded was refused. In 1814 the King of England was empowered by royal warrant to substitute hanging as the ordinary method of executing criminals. Yet beheading remained part of the common law method of dealing with treason as late as 1820: traitors had their heads cut off

by a masked man after they were hanged.
Tony Martin, Nunhead, London SE15.

QUESTION: What was the original 'red herring'?

☐ A RED herring is a smoked herring, or kipper. Its figurative sense derives from the use of kippers as a decoy to draw hounds off a scent. The earliest mention of red herrings recorded in the *OED* is from a cook-book dated 1430, but the *locus classicus* for all scholars of the kipper is that neglected masterpiece, *Nashe's Lenten Stuffe*, published in 1599. Subtitled 'The Prayse Of The Red Herring', this was the last known work by the Elizabethan pamphleteer Thomas Nashe. It is a eulogy of the herring fishermen of Great Yarmouth, where Nashe lived while in exile from London; and of the kipper itself, the 'stuffe' which fed him during this lean period. The figurative sense of the red herring is implicit throughout the book, as a series of rhapsodic tangents or diversions from his theme.
Charles Nicholl, Lower Breinton, Herefordshire.

☐ CHARLES Nicholl is seriously in error when he defines a red herring as 'a smoked herring or kipper'. The kipper is very much with us; the red herring is something of an endangered species. The herring is gutted and opened out flat before smoking to produce a kipper, while the red herring is smoked for far longer periods and retains its uncut fishy form.
C. H. Read, Bradwell, Norfolk.

QUESTION: How did the English court system come to have a 12-person jury?

☐ THE first clause of the Assize of Clarendon in 1166 stated '. . . declarations shall be made for every county and for every hundred by twelve of the more competent men of a hundred'. This is the first recorded statute requiring a jury of 12 in a court of law, but juries had already been in existence for some time – jurors had been widely used during the Domesday Inquest of 1086 to swear to the extent of land-holding before the Domesday Commissioners. It has to be understood that juries at this time were not present to decide on a verdict but were in fact attestors or witnesses. In the royal courts they appeared before the judges to swear that a certain crime had been committed and that the prisoner on trial had been the person who committed that crime. Similar procedures had been current in Anglo-Saxon law and the Norman Conquest had introduced ideas that had been common under Carolingian law in France. It was the Norman kings of England, however, who refined the process and formulated the 12-man jury as an alternative to trial by combat or trial by ordeal: trial by jury became common practice from about 1200. Juries of eight or nine were quite common in the Domesday Inquest, and later Grand Juries could be much larger, but the figure of 12 decided upon for the Anglo-Norman jury seems to rest on a practice common to areas of Lincolnshire around the year 1000 when 'twelve leading thanes of the wapentake' swore they would neither protect the guilty nor accuse the innocent. Other than that, one can only say that 12 has always been a significant mystical number – 12 months, 12 signs of the zodiac, 12 apostles, the duodecimal system devised by the Babylonians, etc.

Colin Pilkington, Burscough, Lancs.

QUESTION: Is evolution a theory still waiting to be proved by the discovery of 'missing links'?

☐ No. EVOLUTION is known to happen; there are sequences of 'links' without missing bits. Moreover, we can see evolution happening. The best-known example is a type of moth in which, originally, most individuals were pale and camouflaged against the bark of birch trees. There were always a few darker individuals. When industrial pollution stained the trees, white moths were easily seen and picked off by birds but dark ones were now well camouflaged. The population evolved from being predominantly white to being predominantly dark. If the questioner was referring more specifically to human evolution, then we scientists must be more careful. Although there are fossils showing parts of the evolutionary pathway, and although there is other evidence (we share something like 98 per cent of our genetic code with chimpanzees), we cannot prove scientifically that humans evolved from something non-human. A belief in evolution is the only known scientific way of making sense of the evidence, but it would be arrogant and unscientific of us to state human evolution as a fact.

Dr Peter Cotgreave, Department of Zoology, Oxford.

☐ LIKE all good scientific theories, this theory is framed in such a way as to be eminently falsifiable: the discovery of the bones of a horse or baboon in the same geological stratum as the remains of a dinosaur, for example, would comprehensively demolish it. Despite this, no such contrary evidence has been found and all that we have learnt from genetics and molecular biology, two sciences unknown to Charles Darwin, has supported the theory – though there is still room for debate about the details (is natural selection the only driving force; is the rate of evolutionary change constant?). Use of the words 'missing link' suggests a fundamental misconception of what the theory states. Evolution cannot be likened to a simple linear process, like a ladder with distinct rungs that have to be slotted in in a particular sequence. A better model would be a continuously branching tree. From this we can see that our nearest biological relatives, the primates, are all as far along their particular branches of the tree as we are

along ours and our relationship to them, from the close to the not-so-close, can be shown directly. The theory does not require a 'link' at some notional man-ape boundary.
Michael Hutton, Camberwell, London SE5.

QUESTION: Does anyone know where the phrase 'the world's oldest profession' to describe prostitution originates? Is it really?

☐ THERE is a similar phrase in the morality play *The Fall of Righteousness* (*c.* 1340). Cain, having been exiled, is wandering in the wilderness when he is visited by Lilith, an agent of Satan. Her function is to explain to him the nature of the post-Fall society he is to encounter and, during her description of this world of sin, she claims: 'Whoredom is the original business of woman.' This should probably be taken less as a statement of fact than as an example of medieval misogyny.
Alwyn W. Turner, London NW5.

☐ A GARDENER, an architect and a politician were discussing which is the oldest profession. 'Horticulture,' said the gardener. 'Who made the Garden of Eden?' 'No,' said the architect. 'It must be architecture, for God created the Earth and the Heavens out of Chaos.' 'Yes,' said the politician, 'but who created the Chaos?'
Anna R. Cooper, Bournemouth.

☐ OF COURSE prostitution is not the world's oldest profession. For 90 per cent of our history, humans have lived as hunter-gatherers, and I have encountered no instance of prostitution in societies organised in this manner. Prostitution is better seen as a recent aberration in human history – though one could argue the same for profession-

alisation. Midwifery is really the world's oldest profession. Shamanism probably runs it a close second; occasionally the two are combined.
Roxana Waterson, Singapore.

QUESTION: Who first 'carried the can'?

☐ THIS derives from the most responsible and critical job in the Army – emptying the latrines.
David Brinicombe, Ealing, London W5.

QUESTION: Exactly when will the world's oil run out, and will there be any alternative convenient energy available at that time?

☐ THE rate of consumption of oil is not constant. Fuel efficiency measures may decrease the rate of consumption, or, more likely, increases in use in less-developed areas will increase the rate of consumption. Also, it is not known exactly how much oil exists. Geographers usually distinguish between a resource – that is, the total amount of oil on the planet – and a reserve, which is the total amount of oil we know about and can extract economically. Clearly, the reserves of oil are always changing with new finds, or improvements in technology, or changes in price. At best, all that can be said is that current reserves at current rates of consumption should last until at least 2030. Undoubtedly, however, oil will run out some day if we continue to use it at anything approaching current rates. Whether we have an alternative depends on many factors. One thought is that as oil becomes more scarce the price will increase, which will force industry and governments to act to find alternatives. The sceptics argue that even if there is sufficient foresight for this to happen, the transition may well be difficult, with increased potential

for conflict as organisations fight (perhaps literally) for the remaining reserves.
Mark Payne, Montacute, Somerset.

☐ REGARDING alternatives, the main uses for which oil is particularly convenient are transportation – uniquely so, in the case of aviation fuel, for which no real substitute has yet been found – and certain grades of lubricants, which as yet have not been recreated synthetically. However, for all other purposes oil is going out of favour, primarily on environmental grounds. In almost all instances, including motor transport, the substitute fuels will be natural gas (methane), which is cheap, plentiful (it exists in greater quantities than oil), safe, and far cleaner than coal or oil.
Nicholas Perry, Croydon.

QUESTION: When did we start the absurd practice of ironing our clothes, and why do we persist with this futile activity?

☐ THE Chinese have used smoothing irons for two millennia, and in royal Korean tombs, *c.* AD 500, was found a box-iron – hot stones were its heat-source. In Europe, the pressing of wet linen had been done with a smooth surface, either weighted or screwed down onto the cold, and probably damp, cloth ('press' as in cider or cheese press). The cloth was folded: the resulting crisp creases can be seen in many paintings. Heated metal irons were essential in tailoring and hat-making to shrink-shape wool cloth: in the 16th century they were used to give the perfect flat finish to the newest status garments, shirts and shifts of linen so fine-spun and woven that its costliness was shown off at neck and wrist. Since ironing is a time-consuming occupation, unwrinkled clothes became, and have remained, the ideal luxury – every

time light linen, or later cotton, fabric is worn it should be washed, and patiently ironed, preferably by laundry-maids, with special instruments for the frills.
Ann MacDonald, London.

☐ IRONING was invented to occupy one's mind while watching television.
John Gray, Norwich.

QUESTION: What is the origin of the phrase 'taking the mickey'?

☐ MICHAEL Barrett was the last man to be publicly hanged in Britain – for an explosion at Clerkenwell Jail in 1867, which was an attempt to free a leader of the Fenians, Richard O'Sullivan Burke. Irish immigrants were to become known as 'Michael Barretts', a term of derision later shortened to 'Micks'. The stereotype of the Irish being stupid gave rise to the term 'taking the mickey'.
David Glinch, London SE6.

☐ ACCORDING to both James Macdonald's *Dictionary of Obscenity, Taboo and Euphemism* (Sphere, 1988) and R. W. Holder's *Dictionary of Euphemisms* (Faber, 1987), 'Mike Bliss' or 'Mickey Bliss' was Cockney rhyming slang, and 'taking the Mickey' was therefore 'taking the piss'. E. J. Burford, in *The Orrible Synne: A Look at London Lechery*. . . (Calder-Boyars, 1973), also reports that 'micgan' was Old English for piss, from the old Norse 'migan', and that this was the root of the expression.
P. Cross, Highbury, London N5.

☐ P. CROSS is right to identify the origin of the phrase in Cockney rhyming slang. However, to suggest that it owes something to the Old English 'micgan' is to overlook the

medical term for the same process, micturition.
Neil Grant, Kings Heath, Birmingham.

QUESTION: Are there any valid arguments, other than religious ones, as to why it would be better for the planet for the human race to continue rather than to become extinct?

☐ THE questioner asks whether or not it would be better for 'the planet'. This is a problem of values. The planet, in so far as it is a material object, clearly has no values of its own, since values are a product of consciousness. The planet could no more experience pleasure in the continued existence of life than it would lament its passing. It therefore follows that any positive attributes the planet is thought to possess only exist because of their presence in the mind of a living being capable of experiencing them. So far as we know, humans are able to experience more complex and varied responses to the world than any other animal. This opinion may be no more than 'speciesist' vanity, but the existence of anything approaching human levels of creative thought in other animals is so far unproven. In any case, whatever other animals think, we can only answer this question from within our own value system. To this extent it answers itself. The beauties and pleasures of the natural world which we experience are only recognised as such because we are here to do the recognising. If we didn't exist, neither would these experiences. The planet is only valuable as long as someone is here to value it. Our existence is thus a necessary condition for the continuation of the planet itself as something which is meaningful.
(Dr) P. Barlow, Sunderland University, Tyne and Wear.

☐ DR BARLOW'S answer is based on the assumption that '*better*' necessarily means '*morally superior*': this makes

nonsense in the context. In the English language it can also mean 'in a superior physical condition', as when we say that someone is better after an illness. In this sense the planet would obviously be better without the human race. In these days of efficient contraception, and when there are few family businesses left to keep going, the main motives for perpetuating the human race must be to satisfy the parental instinct, to attempt to achieve some sort of immortality, or to keep *Debrett's Peerage* in business. However, it may surprise the questioner to know that two Christian sects, the Albigenses and Cathari in the 11th–13th centuries in southern France and elsewhere, condemned procreation on the grounds that it increased the amount of evil in the world which they saw as a battleground between spiritual good and material evil. They were condemned as heretics and became the victims of a crusade led by our Simon de Montfort.
Robert Sephton, Oxford.

☐ IT WAS not *our* Simon de Montfort, Earl of Leicester, born in 1208, who led the merciless crusade against the Albigenses and Cathars in south-west France. It was Simon IV le Fort, Sire de Montfort, who was appointed to lead the crusade in 1209, following the assassination of the Papal Envoy, Pierre de Castelnau, near St Gilles. Meanwhile, *our* Simon de Montfort was a babe in arms.
F. Paul Taylor, Frodsham.

☐ I WONDER if Robert Sephton realises that by introducing the Albigenses and Cathars into the debate, he undermines his own argument. These sects, like other forms of Manicheism, believed that all matter was evil. For them, the world would be a better place if all biological life was extinguished. By this logic, a healthy planet is a dead planet. So keep up the good work, all you polluters out there!
Flavia Dunford-Trodd, Liverpool.

☐ IF IT is acceptable and rational for a parent to step in front of a speeding bullet to save a child, which most people would agree on, then it is also acceptable and rational to wish for my/our extinction in order to save the planet. All one needs to do is give a plausible defence of what one is trying to save. If there are two alternatives – the complete extinction of all life on Earth or the extinction of all human life – which do we choose? According to Dr Barlow, who says that 'the planet is only valuable as long as someone is there to value it', one might as well make the decision with a pin. This I cannot accept. The second alternative leaves the planet intact and with a wealth of biological diversity, whereas the first leaves just another dead planet. There is a difference. The real question is, is this the alternative that faces us?
Giles Radford, Ashford, Kent.

QUESTION: What are the 10 longest novels ever published?

☐ THE novel is generally defined as a piece of fiction, usually in prose form, of about 50,000 words or more. However, we can include works originally published in periodicals – authors such as Dickens and Joyce wrote some novels through them – as well as bound trilogies where the work has a continual singular narrative focus. In the light of this, here are 10 well-known works that may answer the question, though not in any accurate order of size. The first two were found listed in the *Guinness Book of Records*:
1. *Les Hommes de Bonne Volonté* – Louis Frigoule (pp. 4,959).
2. *Tokugawa Ieyasu* – Sohach Yomacka (40 volumes).
3. *A Man Without Quality* – Mussell.
4. *A Dance to the Music of Time* – Anthony Powell.
5. *The Remembrance of Things Past* – Marcel Proust.
6. *Clarissa* – Richardson.
7. *The Wanderer* – F. Burney.

8. *War and Peace* – Tolstoy.
9. *Camilla* – F. Burney.
10. *The Lord of the Rings* – Tolkien.
C. Norton, The Sheffield/Hallam University Literary Society.

☐ IF C. NORTON is right to include trilogies and novel sequences, then surely such works as Laurence Durrell's *Avignon Quartet* (1,367 pages) and Henry Williamson's *Chronicle of Ancient Sunlight* (which he certainly regarded as a single work of fiction) should be allowed. Incidentally, Hugo's *Les Misérables* (1,232 pages) is certainly longer than *The Lord of the Rings* (1,172 pages including appendices).
Nicky Smith, Streatham, London SW2.

☐ LET'S not forget the extraordinary 18th-century Chinese novel *The Story of the Stone* (also known as *The Dream of the Red Chamber*) by Cao Xueqin. This moving, charming novel runs to 2,354 pages in the five-volume Penguin edition – about half as long again as *War and Peace*.
Glenn Oldham, South Ealing, London W5.

QUESTION: What is the origin – etymologically and socio-linguistically speaking – of the word 'spiv'?

☐ THE suggested palindrome seems wide of the mark, particularly as its early usage appears to have been exclusively cockney working-class, usually with criminal connotations. My father, Bill Naughton, besides giving 'spiv' the currency which it enjoyed in the 1940s (thanks mainly to an article of his which appeared in the first issue of Charles Madge's sociological quarterly *Pilot Papers*, and later in the *News Chronicle*), suggested it was an acronym. In a volume of his autobiography, published in 1987 – five years before he died – he wrote: '. . . it was customary for the police from a certain

West End police station to keep that area of London free of tramps and beggars.' A man of disreputable appearance daring to walk around Belgravia would be taken into custody, and described on the charge sheet as 'Suspected Person: Itinerant Vagabond' with the capital letters prominent.
L. M. Naughton, Southgate, W. Sussex.

☐ *BREWER'S Dictionary of Phrase and Fable* says that it is probably an abbreviation of 'spiffing', an old slang word meaning 'fine', 'excellent', an allusion to flash, dandified appearance.
H. G. Hereward, Toller Porcorum, Dorset.

☐ BILL Naughton may have given the word 'spiv' national currency, as your correspondent says, but he was wide of the mark in suggesting it had anything to do with people of disreputable appearance. *Brewer's* guess that it abbreviates 'spiffing' is also unlikely, as that was a public school word never used by cockneys. My recollection is that it came into being among south Londoners during the War and originally meant someone who dressed in a certain flash style in suits tailor-made by a Mr Spivack. Spivacks, or spivs, came to mean civilians who dressed in that style (at the time of the zoot suit in America) and could afford to throw their money around. Bearing in mind wartime conditions, most were petty black market operators, some small-time criminals, sometimes itinerant, but not vagrants. Some spivs carried shivs (knives) so there was also an element of rhyming slang.
A. E. Meltzer, London SE13.

☐ WHEN I was an infant in wartime London, the cavity of my bassinet pram was often used to transport black-market goods around Bermondsey (with me gurgling disarmingly on top). I can therefore state with some authority that SPIVs originated during the Second World War as the characters

who dealt in illicit Supplementary Petrol Issue Vouchers, which were even more precious than nylons.
Ron Birch, Stroud, Gloucs.

QUESTION: What is the origin of the peculiar habit of the clergy of wearing a dog collar?

☐ A DOG collar is a reversed God collar.
Robin Boyes, Scarborough, N. Yorks.

☐ IT GOES back to the arrival in this country of Father Gentili, of the Roman Catholic Order of the Institute of Charity. He came in the 1840s to preach a mission and the habit of his order incorporated a circular collar of the kind now familiar to us. At that time, clergy of all denominations usually wore a white stock but Father Gentili's collar created a vogue, at first among his fellow Catholic priests and later among all clergy. By the end of the century it was in common use. The term 'dog collar' is frequently resented by clerics; it was at first called a 'Roman collar'.
Tony Glynn, Manchester 14.

QUESTION: What happened to Kunzle cakes? During the Sixties they were readily available but now seem to have disappeared.

☐ CHRISTIAN Kunzle was a Swiss chef who settled in Birmingham, making confectionery, chocolates and cakes. Such was his success that Kunzle cakes became known throughout the country and the company opened a number of coffee shops in the Midlands. For many years Kunzles remained a family firm. There are a number of stories of Mr Kunzle sending consumptive factory workers to his holiday home in Switzerland for recuperation. Marks & Spencer wanted

to sell Kunzle cakes under their own name but, despite several approaches, the firm always refused. It was only on the death of Christian Kunzle that the family agreed to supply cakes with the 'St Michael' brand. As managing director of Kunzles, my late grandfather oversaw the sale of the firm in 1962. I believe the catering elements eventually became part of R. S. McColl and the cakes were acquired by Lyons.
Paul Bason, Manchester.

QUESTION: What is, or was, the 'light fantastic' that I have often been urged to do?

☐ A TOE. This corny cliché is taken from Milton's 'L'Allegro'. The poem is a hymn to Mirth – 'thou goddess fair and free' – which starts by consigning 'loathed Melancholy' to a 'dark Cimmerian desert'. Then, after a romp or two among 'fresh blown roses washed in dew', he invites Mirth to 'Come, and trip it as ye go On the light fantastic toe, And in thy right hand lead with thee, The mountain nymph, sweet Liberty.' That's all there is about toes, unless you count a curious reference to 'Jonson's learned sock'. I am rather fond of the poem, for all its extravagant nonsense, but it occurs to me that it made an excellent statement of David Mellor's brief, during his life as Minister for Fun.
Simon Reynolds, Southfields, London SW18.

☐ MILTON liked the phrase and used it again in Cornus: 'Come, knit hands, and beat the ground/ In a light fantastic round'.
Alison Mace, Keighley, Yorks.

QUESTION: From where does the word 'quid' originate?

☐ THE Irish word 'cuid', meaning 'share', is commonly used in phrases such as 'cuid mhaith airgid' – a good deal of money. It is possible that the word transferred to English slang use via Irish-speaking soldiers in the British Army.
Tony Scanlan, Clarinbridge, Co. Galway, Ireland.

☐ *THE Oxford Dictionary of Etymology* gives the origin as 18th-century slang for a sovereign or guinea, derived from the Latin *quid* meaning 'something'. An alternative derivation might be from the French 'quibus', 'the wherewithal'.
Michael Hutton, London SE5.

☐ IT IS a contraction of the Latin phrase 'quid pro quo' which has come to mean a reciprocal agreement. Bank notes carry the wording 'Promise to pay the bearer...' which constitutes such an agreement. Therefore, when £1 notes were the most common variety they became known as 'a quid'.
Robin Webb, Winchester, Hampshire.

QUESTION: When and for what were tickets first issued?

☐ THE first tickets were issued in 1454. They were indulgences granted by Pope Nicholas V to those who gave money to help the campaign against the Turks, who had taken Constantinople the previous year. Indulgences were slips of paper granting remission of the punishment due to sin after absolution. Most from that period were handwritten, but those issued in Mainz were printed (predating the Gutenberg Bible), with blank spaces for the donor's name. Effectively, they were tickets to Heaven.
John Farrow, Dept. of Library and Information Studies, Manchester Metropolitan University.

☐ ALL civilised urban communities would have needed tickets of some kind. In ancient Athens, tickets were needed for admission to the theatre, the law courts, the Assembly, and other places attended by large gatherings of people. There was a small fee for attendance as a juryman at the law courts, or as a voting citizen at the Assembly: this could be obtained on production of one's ticket. The tickets were usually stamped discs of metal or terracotta; a great many have been found, and are described and illustrated in Sir Arthur Pickard-Cambridge's book, *The Dramatic Festivals of Athens*. The earliest surviving specimens date from the end of the fifth century BC.
David Barrett, Oxford.

QUESTION: When, and why, did men first start shaving? At face value, it seems ludicrous to scrape hair off the body every day.

☐ ALEXANDER the Great is responsible. The rationale behind its introduction was that an enemy soldier could gain an advantage by seizing his opponent by the beard. I don't know if there are any records of soldiers being killed in this way in classical times. Mary Ranault, in her book *The Nature of Alexander*, suggests that his real motive was to preserve his own androgynous appearance; the practice then spread to his men.
Alan Dimes, London SW10.

☐ THEY started long before Alexander the Great. He lived in the fourth century BC, but sculptures from the ancient civilisations of Mesopotamia, the Nile and the Indus show that members of the Sumerian, Egyptian and Indian ruling classes were clean-shaven 2,000–3,000 years earlier.
Nicolas Walter, London N1.

QUESTION: What is the most (monetarily) valuable object in the known universe in terms of value per unit mass?

☐ A SUBSTANCE known as Prostaglandin E2 (used in research into respiratory function) is commercially available at a cost of £17.90 per nanogram. This equates to £3,580 billion per kilogram.
John Peacock, Cardiff.

☐ THE *Guinness Book of Records* tells us that, in 1970, the element californium was available for sale at $10 per microgram, approximately £6 billion a kilo. Of course, it's unlikely you could buy a whole kilogram, but if you did you'd probably get a bulk discount.
Mike Frost, Bilton, Rugby.

☐ ATOMS much heavier than uranium do not occur in nature, and have to be made artificially in large accelerators. For the very heaviest elements, literally only a few atoms have been made, with the almost unimaginably small mass of about 0.0000000000000000000002 of a gram per atom. Considering the size of the accelerator and the length of time the scientific teams have worked on it, a million pounds would be a very conservative estimate of their cost, so these atoms are at least five thousand million million million million pounds per gram. This enormously exceeds the annual gross domestic product of the entire world. They only last a tiny fraction of a second before decaying, and for some of them a few grams in one place would cause a nuclear explosion. So if you can afford the price the enjoyment will be short-lived!
Prof. Harvey Rutt, University of Southampton.

☐ A BIRTH certificate bearing the name House of Windsor would be worth several millions sterling per gram.
Roger Nall, Worcester.

QUESTION: Is it true the average height of Britons has increased by a foot or more over the last few centuries? Is this phenomenon caused by improved diet? When will we stop growing?

☐ IN 1873, the medical officer and the natural science master at Marlborough College measured the height of 500 or so of the pupils. At 16½ years the average height of the boys was 65.5 inches. When a comparable sample was measured 80 years later, the average was 69.6 inches – equivalent to a gain of half an inch a decade. James Tanner (in *Foetus into Man*, 1978) makes the point that such trends in children's height are at least partially accountable in terms of earlier maturity. The so-called secular trend at completion of stature in adulthood is in the region of four inches in a hundred years. He did not detect a slowing down in the trend. Although improved standards of nutrition are cited as one possible cause, Tanner also invokes a genetic explanation, which in turn hangs on the increased incidence of marriages and procreation outside the village community. He notes that a key factor in the growth of this 'outbreeding' was the introduction of the bicycle.
Peter Barnes, Milton Keynes.

☐ THE study of skeletons from archaeological excavations has shown that the average height of the population within the British Isles (and elsewhere) has varied over time, and there is no doubt that the single most important influence is that of diet. In this present era of food surpluses and balanced diets in Europe, most people will grow to their full genetic potential (unless other factors such as smoking or ill-health intervene). But earlier generations were acutely prone to the fluctuations of harvests, poverty and starvation – unless they were members of privileged groups. Skeletons of wealthy lay-people found in excavations I directed at Norton Priory in Cheshire showed their height to be little different in range to that of the present-day population. The peasant

population of the same era tended not to grow as tall, and would usually die much younger.
Dr Patrick Greene, Director, Museum of Science and Industry in Manchester.

☐ AVERAGE young male height around 1750 was about 160 cm (63 inches) and in 1980 it was 176 cm (69.3 inches); there is no evidence of growth as large as another 6 inches in earlier centuries. The answer is complex because there has always been significant variation in height between social classes, although the inequality has narrowed over time; it therefore matters whom you measure. The average height of public school boys has risen less than that of working-class children. This fact helps to answer the second question: the primary cause of growth is increased income, which means that people can eat more, although changes in disease and pollution can have effects. But it also means that the increased income inequality since 1979 may be affecting average heights and variation between classes. We do not know when we will stop growing; in Britain we still have a long way to go to catch up with richer nations such as the Netherlands, where young males average over 180 cm (71 inches).
Roderick Floud (co-author Height, Health and History *CUP), London Guildhall University.*

☐ LET'S assume that there have been humans or human-like beings for some 2 million years or, say, 100,000 generations. If their average height increased each generation by a mere one-thousandth of an inch we should now be 8 ft 4 inches taller than our remote ancestors. It seems therefore that there are powerful influences restricting humans to a fairly narrow variation in height, even over long periods of time.
Louis Judson, Penrith, Cumbria.

QUESTION: Are we still evolving or is this as good as we get?

☐ THE advent of genetic engineering will allow us to fast-forward the rate of evolution and shape our progeny according to our whims. Regardless of whether this is desirable, it is uncontrollable and only a matter of time before this technology transforms humanity. Some scientists such as Hans Moravec go even further, and suggest that a 'genetic takeover' is under way, where artificial computerised life-forms will start to evolve faster than their organic counterparts. Aided by us and unfettered by biological constraints, these programs will develop intelligence in advance of our own. Rather than being wiped out by our creations, we will be able to copy our brain patterns on to computers and transcend our bodies, 'becoming' these cybernetic super-beings.
Chris Mungall, Edinburgh.

☐ No ANSWER is possible. Evolution is a classic example of a chaotic process – with a touch of catastrophe theory thrown in. Each micro-step is rational, but the future state is unpredictable from any knowledge we can attain of the present state. We can, of course, speculate. We could say that man is a recent arrival on the scene, embodying exciting new developments, with lots of potential. He lacks features which species that have been around for significant evolutionary time have – for example, the ability to control his population – but these deficiencies may be balanced by his ability to use intelligent behaviour to solve physiological problems in a fraction of the time biological adaptation would take. On the other hand, the current view is that evolution proceeds in surges that follow mass extinctions caused by such events as comets hitting the earth. It is not too difficult to imagine that the next mass extinction may be due to human action and will include man. That would not actually be unprecedented. When algae discovered photosynthesis and filled

the earth's atmosphere with oxygen, pre-existing anaerobic organisms, had they been articulate, must have described this as a dreadful catastrophe, and they ceased to be the dominant life-forms. We, however, looking back, see the event as 'good'. There seems to be a principle at work, which we do not understand, that causes physical and biological evolution to proceed towards greater complexity and in some sense 'forward'. (St Paul had the insight that 'All things are moving towards perfection.') I think our knowledge of the earth's history justifies optimism, whatever the future of our particular species.
Prof. Romaine Hervey, Wells, Somerset.

□ IF THERE were an ice age next week, with massive crop failures, famines and a general 'collapse of civilisation', then you can be certain that evolutionary pressures would once again come to bear. People more able to tolerate the cold (large and fat?) would be more likely to survive to breeding age; very hairy men (and women), who might be sexually unattractive now, would quickly establish a foothold in the gene pool.
David Gibson, Leeds.

QUESTION: What is the universe expanding into?

□ THE simple answer is 'itself'. The universe is all there is, it has *no outside*. This is not the same as saying 'there is nothing outside', since that requires a boundary and the universe is boundless. The commonest metaphor used to try to visualise this is the child's balloon. The rubber of an inflating balloon expands, every point on it gets further from every other. Yet to a two-dimensional population living in its surface their world is not expanding *into* anything, it is mysteriously getting bigger. Of course, with this analogy

of the universe, the big bang comes at the wrong end!
Patrick O'Neill, Eastleigh, Hants.

☐ IT IS not a vacuum, since that is inside the universe and is traversed by electrical, magnetic and gravitational fields. So one could describe the space beyond the boundary of the universe as nothing – a lack of anything except, perhaps, thought of conscious beings. Matter expanding into 'nothing' at the boundary of the universe will have a negative electrical charge because this is repelled by radiation pressure and will accelerate much more than relatively heavy matter with positive charges. This produces an increasing potential gradient, and eventually immense electrical discharges form huge jets of positively charged matter which condense to form the strings of galaxies we can now observe with our sophisticated telescopes and even binoculars. Most of the current 'mysteries' of astronomy can be explained without postulating bizarre ideas about so-called black holes and cosmic strings.
Eric Crew, Broxbourne, Herts.

QUESTION: At what stage in cinema history were the simple words 'The End' replaced by four miles of credits that about four people stay behind to read? And why?

☐ I CAN remember when 'The Queen' was played at the end of every cinema showing, prompting a disorderly rush to get out before the end of the credits, and the habit has stayed. Credits are primarily an ego trip but also help when negotiating fees and have an effect on residual payments. Television has solved the problem of self-multiplying credits by spooling them past too fast to read, but the cinema has more time to spare and they help to get the punters out. The four people who stay behind may be

looking for the names of friends or colleagues, but are more likely proclaiming their supposed Show Business membership to the other three.
David Brinicombe, retired Film Sound Recordist, Ealing, London.

☐ THIS dates from the demise in the Sixties of the dream-factory studio system. In that era, the functions and services which are now so laboriously listed were simply part of the fixed infrastructure of the studio operation, and the persons performing them were salaried employees working in a relatively secure and stable environment. In those circumstances they had no incentive to claim on-screen credits. Now, the studios have essentially become rental facilities, with the infrastructure fragmented into competing contracted-out service providers; thus even caterers are only as good as their last round of sandwiches and need credits to survive in their competitive world.
Bernard Hrusa-Marlow, Morden, Surrey.

☐ CLOSING credits on films are treated with proper respect in Paris, where cinema is an art form. However long they may last, they are sat through reverently by Parisians who vocally deprecate the indecent haste with which Anglo-Saxon visitors make for the exits.
Henry Cleere, Paris.

QUESTION: What is the origin of the 'Jack' in Union Jack, and under what circumstances is the Union Jack flown on board ship?

☐ THE Union Jack consists of the Union Flag bordered all round with a narrow white border. It is flown from the jack-staff in the eyes of the bows of Royal Navy ships, and in this place only. It is never flown ashore. What is flown from public

buildings and private houses is properly known as the Union Flag, which is never flown at sea.
L. W. Hammond, Sudbury, Suffolk.

☐ L. W. HAMMOND was a bit over-pedantic. The Union Jack is flown on Royal Navy ships as a mark of nationality. It is also worn on any ship carrying an Admiral of the Fleet or on which a court-martial is taking place, and was at one time part of the range of signals used by the Navy. For these reasons it cannot be used as a national flag by civilian vessels, which have to use the Red Ensign. Civilian vessels can, however, use the Union Jack with a white border as described by Mr Hammond (the one used by the Navy has no white border). There is no law that says the plain flag when used on land has to be called the Union Flag – that is simply a custom which grew up in the Army. Scouts, Guides and the Government itself have referred to the flag as the Union Jack for a long time, and the name has become established as an affectionate nickname for our national flag, both on land and at sea. As to the origins of the term, the answer is that nobody knows. Some attribute it very speculatively to King 'Jacques' in whose reign it was introduced, although why his name has to be rendered in French is left unexplained. Others think that 'jack' is a term for a small version of an object. From about 1630 the flag began to be flown from the bowsprit rather than from the mainmast of a naval vessel, and it is possible that it received its name at that time. The first recorded instance of the term is in 1633. The following year Sir Nathaniel Boteler, referring to the flag, wrote: 'Every such vessel . . . is permitted and enjoined to wear one of these in a small volume in her bowsprit's top.' That has been the case ever since.
William G. Crampton, Director, The Flag Institute, Chester.

☐ I AM afraid L. W. Hammond was incorrect. The Union

Flag with a white border is the Pilot Jack which may be worn by any British-registered ship in harbour and wearing her ensign. It is, in fact, very rarely seen.
Robert Moore, Holywell, Clwyd.

QUESTION: If Essex, Sussex, Wessex and Middlesex belonged to Saxons in the east, south, west and middle respectively, what happened to the Saxons in the north?

☐ THEY lived in Nosex, so they all died out.
Malcolm Brown, Glasgow; Peter Mair, Netherlands; Helena Corran, Bath; and many more . . .

☐ THE questioner is overestimating the importance of the South Saxons. In the historic period after the initial Anglo-Saxon invasions, Sussex was largely ignored as an unimportant backwater. After an initially fierce invasion which led the South Saxon king Aelle to be recognised as overlord of all the English, Sussex seemed to have been rigidly contained within not very extensive boundaries and rapidly sank from sight – the Anglo-Saxon Chronicle does not mention Sussex between 491 and 675. By the time Sussex was conquered by Offa of Mercia in the eighth century, the South Saxons were divided up and owing allegiance to at least three local kinglets. At the time the Anglo-Saxon kingdoms were being formed in the middle of the sixth century, the Saxons were basically divided into the West Saxons and the East Saxons. At some earlier point there had been a people occupying the land to the west of London who, from their position between the West and East Saxons, were known as Middle Saxons. But, by the late sixth century, Middlesex north of the Thames had been absorbed with London into Essex, while Middlesex south of the Thames (southern district, Surrey) was disputed between Wessex and Kent. The 'middle' in Middlesex therefore refers to

midway between east and west. In any case, the Angles of
Mercia began beyond Watford.
Colin Pilkington, Ormskirk, Lancs.

**QUESTION: The word 'tragedy' originates from the
Greek words *tragos* (goat) + *oide* (song). How did the
modern meaning evolve?**

☐ HAVE you heard a goat sing?
Marcus Roome, Clapton, London E5.

☐ GREEK tragedies were known as 'goat-songs', because the
prize in Athenian tragedy competitions was a live goat. These
contests were sacred to Dionysos, one of whose animal
incarnations was the goat.
Susanna Roxman, Lund, Sweden.

**QUESTION: When I die, I do not want any memorial or
final resting place. I also don't want to burden my
dependants with the unnecessary expense of a funeral.
What is the cheapest, legal way to dispose of a human
body in England?**

☐ YOU could leave your body to a medical school for dis-
section by students. The snag is that they tend to accept only
bodies that are unautopsied after death, non-cancerous and
within easy range of a school. If your next of kin are receiving
either income support, housing benefit, disability working
allowance or council tax benefit, the local Social Security will
pay for a basic funeral. If not, your relatives can refuse to
arrange for disposal of your body, in which case the local
authority is legally obliged to register the death and carry out
the funeral, with reimbursement from the estate or next of
kin where possible. Your body can be buried by friends and

relatives in a garden or farm with the permission of the landowner, without permission from the council planning department or the environmental health department. It is advisable for the burial to be 250 metres from any human-consumption water supply or well or borehole, 30 metres from any other spring and 10 metres from any field drain, with no water in the grave when first dug. But a garden burial could severely reduce the value of a property. In my view, the most satisfactory option is burial organised by the relatives in a nature reserve burial ground run by a farmer, local authority or wildlife trust, where a tree is planted instead of having a headstone.
Nicholas Albery, Director, Natural Death Centre, London NW2.

☐ BECOME the owner of a privatised mine.
Henry Hubbal, Redditch, Worcester.

☐ THE body should be giftwrapped and left overnight on the back seat of an unlocked car. It will be gone by morning. Failing that, try mailing it Recorded Delivery. This guarantees it'll be lost for ever.
Garry Chambers, London N3.

QUESTION: Why do we 'pull someone's leg'? Why not an arm?

☐ THOMAS Hood wrote in his poem 'The Last Man' (1827):
> I must turn my cup of sorrow quite up,
> And drink it to the dregs,
> For there is not another man alive,
> In the world to pull my legs!

He was referring to the fact that, before the invention of the long drop in executions by hanging, the friends of the criminal were permitted to pull his legs in order to shorten

his suffering. This developed into a sick joke that one's friends would always be around to pull one's legs if needed.
Brian Palmer, Noke Side, Herts.

QUESTION: What is the origin of the term 'gravy train'?

☐ *Brewer's Twentieth Century Phrase and Fable* says that the expression probably goes back to the early years of the century in America. Railroad workers could find a soft run that did not strain them very much. Thus 'gravy', already a slang word for money, was readily added to the railway to make 'riding on the gravy train' a natural expression for them. The *OED* says that American speech has it listed in 1927 as 'a sinecure' and gives the first quoted reference of the phrase to Mary McCarthy in 1952 in *Groves of Academe*.
Len Snow, Wembley, Middlesex.